Camping
ALASKA AND
CANADA'S YUKON

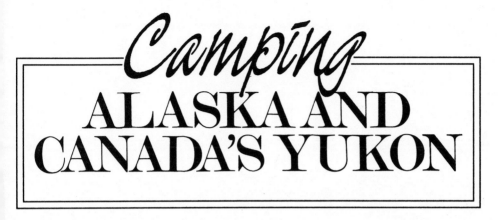

Camping
ALASKA AND
CANADA'S YUKON

The Motorist's Handbook to North Country Campgrounds and Roadways

by Mike and Marilyn Miller

Pacific Search Press

Pacific Search Press
222 Dexter Avenue North
   Seattle, Washington 98109
© 1987 by Mike and Marilyn Miller. All rights reserved
Printed in the United States of America

Edited by Billie Greenhalgh
Designed by Judy Petry
Maps and illustrations by Ed Mills

Cover: Mount McKinley, Alaska. Photograph by Tim Thompson. Inset by
   David Stoecklein/West Stock.

Library of Congress Cataloging-in-Publication Data

Miller, Mike
   Camping Alaska and Canada's Yukon.

   Bibliography: p.
   Includes index.
   1. Camp sites, facilities, etc.—Alaska. 2. Camp
sites, facilities, etc.—Yukon Territory. 3. Automobiles—Road guides—Alaska. 4. Automobiles—Road
guides—Yukon Territory. 5. Alaska—Description and
travel—1981-   —Guide-books. 6. Yukon Territory—
Description and travel—Guide-books. I. Miller,
Marilyn, 1930 Nov. 13-   II. Title.
GV191.42.A4M55   1987   647'.94798   86-30631
ISBN 0-931397-17-0

Contents

Preface

S o you are planning a camping trip to Alaska and Canada's Yukon? Fantastic! You are about to embark on one of North America's most memorable vacation experiences.

No, make that one of earth's most memorable vacation experiences. The trip you have in mind is literally world class: in a category with crossing the Atlantic on the *Queen Elizabeth II*, or in an earlier era with a rail journey on the Orient Express.

Here is what you have to look forward to.

Cloud-piercing mountains and ice-blue glaciers so numerous they have not even all been named yet ... Fishing and hunting so superb the record books are forced to accept new entries each year ... Parks, preserves, refuges, forests, and wilderness areas on a scale so huge they dwarf their counterparts in the lower forty-eight states. Plus modern cities, small towns, roadside lodges, and primitive villages all peopled with Alaskans and Yukoners anxious to bid you welcome. These are only some of the wonders of a North Country vacation you will savor and relive for the rest of your life.

The magnificence of the North Country has caused many of us to set down roots and raise our families here. This is how it happened to us.

The two of us, husband and wife, came north out of Kansas in 1954. Alaska was still a territory then. We both landed jobs working for *The Alaska Sportsman*, a magazine published at that time in Ketchikan. Initially we looked upon our work as something akin to a subsidized vacation, and our plan was to move on to other parts of the nation and the world just as soon as we began to tire of Alaska and its southeastern panhandle.

Alas, more than three decades have now passed and the excitement of being a part of what is now the state of Alaska continues to grow. We are beginning to suspect we may never tire of living, hiking, camping, fishing, and traveling here and in the neighboring Yukon Territory.

Camping has been especially rewarding. Over the years we have camped in trailers, vans, and motorhomes, even bicycle-and-tent camped, along virtually every major highway in this part of the continent.

In the process we have thrilled to the distant, wailing call of wolves during brief hours of summer darkness. We have stood, mouths agape, and marveled at the strength of a grizzly bear scooping roots from concrete-hard packed earth as effortlessly as you would run your finger through a puddle of water. We have giggled out loud at the sight of awkward, gangly moose calves whose features only a mother moose could love. We have held our breath as we watched the thundering spectacle of icebergs the size of office buildings calving off of a glacier face.

Now these same—and perhaps more glorious—experiences await you. It is a trip you will never regret. And never stop remembering.

Alaska, in the language of native Aleutian Islanders, means "the Great Land." When your trip is over, you will understand why.

Mike and Marilyn Miller
Juneau
Spring 1987

Acknowledgments

So many people, now friends and colleagues, have helped in the preparation and research of this book it would be impossible, we regret to say, to list them all. Among the many who provided information and verified data are city and borough (county) clerks, chamber of commerce employees, convention and visitor bureau managers and staff, federal and state agency public information officers, and many, many others. Our debt to all of these fine people is incalculable.

The exceptional labors of a few individuals, however, call for special recognition.

Specifically, we owe great thanks to Neil Johannsen, the capable and cooperative director of Alaska State Parks division in the state Department of Natural Resources. Thanks, too, are due that division's very knowledgeable operations chief Pete Panarese who answered countless questions and supplied us with much, much data; and to the division's southcentral associate regional manager Michel Lee who took over the task of helping us when Pete left to go mountain climbing in the Soviet Union.

Out in the field, Alaska State Parks personnel who gave of their time and expertise included Al Meiners, northern regional manager in Fairbanks; Dale Bingham, area superintendent for Copper Basin and Matanuska-Susitna; Roger Laber, area superintendent for the Kenai Peninsula; and Linda Kruger, manager of Alaska State Parks' southeast region. For years, Linda has been for us an Especially Reliable Resource Person and she continued in that role as we developed this project.

Equally cooperative and helpful has been the Alaska Division of Tourism, headed by Don Dickey who is certainly among the most amiable tourism directors in the nation. Don and his sharp staffers Bill Marchese and John Pearson were of immense help in compiling the latest in general travel information about Alaska as well as specific camping material. Bill Schafer of the Alaska Marine Highway system was similarly a lifesaver by providing and verifying details about travel on Alaska's superb state ferries.

Across the Canada border (surely the friendliest boundary in the annals of international relations) Tourism Yukon's energetic publicity officer Kevin Shackell provided not only plenty of solid, practical information, he was good enough to reread and reverify it after we incorporated it in our book.

And who says federal bureaucrats are stuffy and, well, bureaucratic? Pamela Finney at the United States Forest Service information center in Juneau proved as cordial as she was informative about campgrounds and facilities in Tongass National Forest. Carolyn Dunaway, of the USFS in Anchorage, likewise provided us with all the data we needed about the Chugach National Forest in southcentral Alaska. Similar good grist for our mill came from the Bureau of Land Management's Rich Hagan and from National Park Service's Jim Shives.

Also, our thanks to Betty Oyster of Number One Motorhome Rentals of Alaska, who assisted us mightily in our latest camping foray through Alaska and Canada's Yukon.

To all of these fine folk we extend our deepest thanks. We could never have produced this guide without them.

1

Getting Ready
is Part of the Fun

We were talking, some years back, to a veteran of half a dozen motoring vacations to the North Country. "The worst trip I ever made to Alaska and the Yukon," he said, *"was terrific."*

Your trip will be terrific too. The great, sprawling expanse of diverse lands, the equally diverse but uniformly friendly people, the wildlife, the fishing, even the North Country's unique brand of city life ... these are the ingredients of an Alaska-Yukon journey that bring people north for a once in a lifetime experience, then bring them back time and time again.

RV travelers are especially able to enjoy the very best that the north has to offer. As we will note in the section on Alaska Highway travel, this is still largely wild and frontier country. Traveling, however, on good roads and camping at comfortable campgrounds, you can savor the wilderness, even surround yourself in it; yet you are safe, warm, dry, and completely at ease.

To help you achieve that goal, descriptions of every public campground in Alaska and the Yukon, and the roads that lead to them, begin in Chapter 2. The best features, and the drawbacks, of all these campgrounds and parks are laid out for your consideration in choosing where you want to camp each night during your sojourn in the north.

But first we need to cover some basics. And that is what this initial chapter is all about.

To begin with we offer a very short course in Alaska and Yukon Territory geography—to sort of whet your appetite for more knowledge about the various and varied locales you will see here. Then we list a lot of things you should know and things you should do before actually setting out on your journey. Finally, we make some routing suggestions—which you should feel free to adopt as is, adapt to your individual needs, or totally ignore.

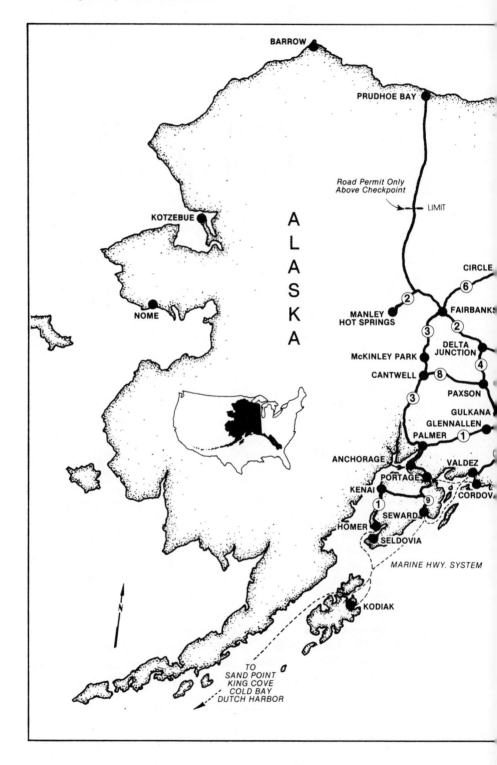

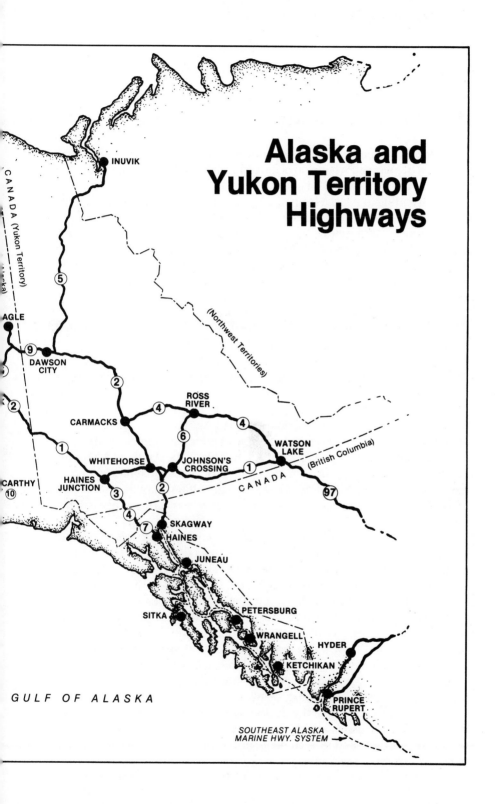

Alaska and Yukon Territory Highways

INUVIK

CANADA (Yukon Territory)

(Northwest Territories)

(5)

AGLE

(9)
DAWSON
CITY

(2)

(2)

ROSS
RIVER

(4)

(4)

CARMACKS

(6)

WATSON
LAKE

(British Columbia)

(1)

WHITEHORSE

JOHNSON'S
CROSSING

(1)

CARTHY

(10)

HAINES
JUNCTION

(3)

(2)

CANADA

(97)

(4)

(7)

SKAGWAY

HAINES

JUNEAU

PETERSBURG

SITKA

WRANGELL

HYDER

KETCHIKAN

GULF OF ALASKA

PRINCE
RUPERT

SOUTHEAST ALASKA
MARINE HWY. SYSTEM →

Alaska's Geography

One of the inescapable facts about Alaska and the Yukon, and it hits you like a tire wrench when you begin seriously thinking about a vacation in the North Country, is that "it's really huge up there."

Just getting to Alaska from many parts of the United States or Canada can take a week or more of driving. From Seattle to Anchorage, for example, is a whopping 2,435 miles. Once you arrive in one part of Alaska there are still vast distances between cities and sites you will want to see. From Anchorage, Homer lies 226 miles away on the Kenai Peninsula. From Anchorage to Haines, just north of Juneau in southeastern Alaska, it is 653 miles. From Whitehorse, Yukon Territory, on the Alaska Highway to Inuvik on the Dempster Highway, it is 814 miles.

All of which means, of course, that a carefree trip to Alaska and Canada's Yukon takes a certain amount of planning.

But far from being a hassle, planning your trip will be half the fun. And "boning up" will make your trip tremendously more enjoyable once you get here.

You will learn in advance, for instance, that there are no Eskimos native to the southeastern panhandle region of Alaska. Do not get off a ferry or cruise ship expecting to see them. Southeast is Indian country. By the same token, do not look in the Arctic for totem poles. The Arctic *is* where the Eskimos live, but they do not carve totems. These magnificent cedar monuments are a southeastern Alaska Indian cultural expression. And do not look *anywhere* in Alaska for snow and ice igloos. You simply will not find any.

So, assignment number one in planning your trip north is to read up about this huge subcontinent. Chapter 7 contains a list of books you will find helpful. In the meantime, here is a thumbnail sketch of regions in Alaska and the Yukon, presented in the order in which they occur in this book.

Southeastern Alaska. Your most vivid memories of southeastern Alaska will be water, mountains, and lush green forests. You will encounter great gobs of all three. Mostly, the region is made up of thousands of big and little islands set to the west of a few miles of coastal mainland. (Beyond the Alaska coastlands eastward is British Columbia, Canada.) No conventional roads connect the cities and villages of southeastern Alaska. Instead you get around here by ferry, cruise ship, or by air.

Gold was the reason the region was peopled soon after Alaska's purchase from Russia in 1867. Today, commercial salmon fishing, timbering, tourism, and government (in the capital city, Juneau) are the principal economic mainstays.

As you ply the sheltered waters of the panhandle, spruce-covered mountains rise up beside you to clouded heights. Fishing craft, both commercial and sport, are frequent companions as you wind your way through the Inside Passage to Ketchikan, Wrangell, Petersburg, Sitka, Juneau, Haines, and Skagway. Natives of the area are coastal Indians who are anxious to share their totemic artistry and their dancing talents.

Yukon Territory. This is still frontier country, a land of prospectors, miners, and homesteaders. Located in the northwesternmost corner of Canada, the territory contains awesome landscapes, abundant wildlife, and an exciting Klondike gold rush heritage that comes to life as you explore the countryside. The Yukon Territory abuts British Columbia to the south, the Northwest Territories to the east, Alaska to the west, and the Arctic Ocean to the north.

Principal cities in the Yukon are Whitehorse, the territory's capital; and Dawson City, the gold rush site on the Klondike river that drew tens of thousands of stampeders beginning in 1897. Seeing stern-wheel riverboats, authentic frontier saloons, and mining sites of the gold rush era ... cruising or canoeing the storied Yukon River ... hiking and backpacking in the Yukon's superb wilderness Kluane National Park ... motoring over the rolling hills and mountains ... these are the features that attract today's visitor-stampeders. Few, if any, are disappointed in what they find here.

Interior Alaska. Where Canada's Yukon ends, Alaska's Interior region begins, and the appeal is much the same. There are miles upon miles of rolling, forested hills and mountains. Lakes and creeks and streams abound: some of them still so untouched, untrammeled, and unsullied that Congress has designated them national wild and scenic rivers. Roaming the woods and tundra are moose, caribou, grizzly bears, and wolves. Sharing their domain are the indomitable homesteaders, prospectors, miners, and no small number of loners who simply seek a small portion of solitude.

Much of Interior Alaska lies in a number of national parks, preserves, wildlife refuges, and wilderness areas; designations that seek to perpetuate the land as it now is, so that future generations will be able to enjoy the same unspoiled land you are visiting.

Fairbanks is the hub center of the Interior. Denali National Park and Preserve and Mount McKinley (at 20,320 feet North America's highest peak) together comprise the region's number one visitor attraction. Trade, the University of Alaska, mining, petroleum, the United States military, and tourism are the Interior's principal dollar producers.

Southcentral Alaska. This is the region where half of Alaska's people live and play. Here at the top of the Gulf of Alaska, shielded by the Alaska Range from Arctic and Interior winter weather extremes, southcentral Alaska contains great glaciers, forests, fertile river valleys, and mountains. Anchorage is by far Alaska's largest city. Other notable communities include Palmer in the rich farmlands of the Matanuska Valley, Seward on the shores of Resurrection Bay, Homer on the tip of the Kenai Peninsula, along with Valdez and Cordova among the fjords of Prince William Sound.

Petroleum is the major industry of southcentral Alaska. You see it in the eight-hundred-mile-long trans-Alaska pipeline that descends from the Arctic at Prudhoe Bay to Southcentral's Valdez harbor. You see it as well in the offshore drilling rigs in the waters of Cook Inlet and in the petrochemical plants nearby. You see it even more plainly in many of Anchorage's multistoried office buildings housing the major oil companies located here. Important in the economic scheme of things, too, are trading, commercial fishing, military bases, the visitor industry, and farming.

Arctic Alaska and the Southwestern Region. Unless you leave your vehicle parked in Anchorage or Fairbanks you will not be able to see these regions of Alaska: gold rush Nome on Norton Sound, arctic Kotzebue, Eskimo Barrow, Prudhoe Bay where the big oil discoveries were made, and the Pribilof Islands clear out in the middle of the Bering Sea. These and other really mind-blowing destinations are accessible only by air.

We recommend them highly. On the shores of the Pribilofs you will see literally thousands of fur seals, the largest such concentrations on earth. At King Island Village near Nome you may buy intricately carved ivory items direct from the artists who lovingly sculpt them. In Kotzebue you will witness the fabled Eskimo blanket toss, and you can even take a turn in the walrus-hide blanket if you wish. At Barrow you can stand on shore and know that there is no place more northerly on the North American continent. Even in such far-out locales, however, accommodations and services are clean, modern, and convenient. Your meals will be strictly "American" in content and cuisine. But if you get the chance, do sample at least a tiny bite of muktuk (raw meat from the bowhead whale). Its taste is subtle and it takes a long, long time to chew; but you will never buy the likes of it at your local grocer's.

These then, in very broad terms, are the various regions of Alaska and the Yukon. Here are some other things you should be aware of, and some things you should do, before you actually start out on your journey.

Preparing Your RV

As you might imagine, a trip to and through Alaska and the Yukon requires more than the usual vehicle preparation. You will be driving on gravel at least part of the time. Highway construction detours are inevitable and they are rougher, more primitive than you may be used to in the lower forty-eight states and Canadian provinces. You will frequently be some distance from service stations and repair facilities.

Do not worry. With a little forethought and preparation before you leave home you can have your rig in shape to handle any situation that might arise. Remember, thousands of motorists travel to Alaska each year, and the number who run into difficulty is very small. They are the people, for the most part, who failed to make common-sense preparations.

For the following list of things you should do to ready your RV, we are much obliged to Dave Stevens, president of Alaska-Yukon RV Caravans. Dave's company is a leader in the field of escorted RV caravaning in Alaska. It is the only such firm that is headquartered here. (See page 26, Travel Options.) His list of things you should do to your vehicle before leaving home, and of things you should bring with you on your trip, is an outgrowth of thousands of hours and miles of RV caravaning in the North Country.

Dave's list of preparations covers almost any eventuality one could anticipate. Our observation is that most Alaska resident RV vacationers do not prepare their units as extensively as Dave recommends, and they probably return home from most trips none the worse for not having done so. However, we would wager that Dave's clients unquestionably suffer fewer breakdowns, by far, than travelers who do not do the preparation work he recommends. Here, from the manual he issues to all participants on his trips, are his suggestions.

Water System. Have your water system checked out prior to leaving for Alaska. Make sure the water pump is in good working order, and that you have a spare. If the potable water holding-tank drain valve is in an area that could be damaged by rocks, protect it with a small metal deflecting shield. Generally this precaution is necessary only if the valve is located on the underside of the rig. A spare valve is optional.

Electrical System. A good battery is essential for your Alaska needs. Have the system checked out to ensure that the battery for your RV auxiliary power receives a charge when the vehicle is running. Also, check the converter to make sure auxiliary power receives a charge when hooked up to power.

You will need an adapter to plug into 110 power; no other adapter is necessary. We do not recommend carrying extra batteries unless they are hooked into the system. Should your battery fail there are ample sources for a new one. It is far too dangerous having a battery bouncing around. If you have a rig with a generator, have the unit checked and serviced prior to leaving for Alaska.

Oil, air filter, and fuel filter should be serviced. Bring along spare plugs. Also bring an extra air filter and plan to install it halfway through your trip.

LP Gas System. Check your rig for the type of piping used in construction. Exposed copper piping should be protected. A very good method is to cover the pipe with garden hose. This protects the system from flying rocks, which can smash the lines flat. *It happens!*

Also, exposed gas valves should be protected by the use of a small deflector, as used with sewer/gray water valves. Have the system checked out completely, test for leaks, and make sure the furnace is in good working order. Nights are cool and you will want to use it.

Sewer/Gray Water Valves. Depending on the type of rig and the location of the valves, precautions vary. For rigs in which the valves are partially enclosed, complete the enclosure and seal the compartment to protect the area from being filled with mud and/or gravel. Stuffing cracks with spun fiberglass or sealing seams with a silicone caulk will work well.

On rigs that have an exposed valve, a light metal deflector shield should be positioned to protect it from damage by rocks. Those towing a trailer or fifth wheel should have heavy mud guard flaps on the tow vehicle. This will also prevent a tremendous amount of small dings to the front and underbelly of your rig.

Other Systems and Appliances. Prior to the beginning of your trip, make sure all gas units, refrigerator, furnace, stove, water heater, and other appliances work as they were designed to do. Avoid bringing something "jerry-rigged." Your twelve-volt power system should function properly to provide lights, fans, pumps, etc.

Dust Protection—Outside Compartments. No RV can be totally protected against dust infiltration. Motorhomes, however, do seem to fare better. The following guidelines should be followed for all rigs.

Outside compartments that are also accessible from inside the rig should be secured against dust infiltration. Depending on the need for accessibility, areas should be stuffed with spun fiberglass. After access is gained and before travel each day, compartments should be taped with duct tape. Purchase your duct tape at home, as prices are extremely high in Alaska and the Yukon due to the great demand. We suggest two large-size rolls. You will use tape daily to cover keyholes, locks, compartments, and hatches.

Refrigerator Compartment. The refrigerator compartment should also be protected. The best way to do this is simply to cover the back side of the hatch door with plastic, such as a garbage bag. Secure it with duct tape. Turn the refrigerator off when moving. If you average only 125 to 150 miles a day it will not get too warm. Then, when you are in camp, open the refrigerator door a couple of inches and turn it on.

Generator Compartment. If your rig has a generator, it should also be protected. The underside can be secured by wiring on a furnace filter to protect the opening. The hatch should be protected, and used, in the same manner as the refrigerator compartment.

Ceiling Fans. Trailers and fifth wheels tend to have a few more problems than other vehicles. However, these additional precautions will ensure a pleasurable experience.

Reverse one of the ceiling vents and install a one-quarter-inch-thick foam filter the size of the opening. When you travel, crack the vent slightly to allow air to be forced into the rig. This creates a back pressure and reduces dust infiltration. If you have storm windows, install them. For those without storm windows there is help in the form of a 3M Company product. It is a window kit that comes ready to install; all you need are scissors and a hair dryer. Check your local hardware store.

You may also tape exterior windows at joints and edges. Depending on the type of rig, if windows are set in, caulking the frame with a silicone caulk will provide excellent protection yet it is easy to remove.

Rock Protection. Even though travel in the north is now mostly on hard surface roads, conditions can still create a lot of flying material—from your own RV as well as trucks and other vehicles. These basic precautions should be followed.

On the front of a vehicle, headlight protectors are a must. Generally these will not be available in stores in the lower forty-eight states. If your local auto parts store does not have them, do not worry. You will be able to purchase them once you arrive in northern British Columbia, the Yukon, or Alaska. The grill area in front of the radiator should be protected with a bug screen or hardware cloth. This will protect the radiator from flying rocks. If mounted properly it may also protect the headlights and lower portion of the windshield. The area surrounding the underside of the rig, which allows air flow for the radiator, must not be blocked, but must be screened.

It is advisable to have adequate insurance to cover the replacement of your front windshield. Without a doubt you will pick up at least one chip or crack, if not more. Trying to cover the windshield proves to be more trouble than it is worth. *Do not* attempt to mount a Plexiglas shield on, over, or around the windshield. You will be in violation of vehicle laws.

Rigs that have a front window up top should protect the glass from rock breakage. Least expensive is the use of cardboard secured by duct tape. It may also be wise to put masking tape X's on the inside of the overhead window. This will protect against flying glass should a rock penetrate the protective cover.

Rigs that have wrap-around front windows and roadside windows immediately back of the front corner should have protection as well. The use of sponge, taped to the window and then covered by visqueen, will provide excellent protection.

Travel Trailers/Fifth Wheels. On the front of your rig it is best to provide protection with the use of three-eighths-inch plywood. On trailers, notch the plywood to fit over the tongue of the trailer, right against the front. Plywood should be fashioned to fit under the front window rock guard. This will help hold it in place. Generally, you are able to remove the plastic insert tape in the corner molding on the trailer. Remove existing screws (one or two) and using the same hole secure the plywood to the front of the trailer. Plastic insert tape should be fine if left partially inserted and secured behind the plywood. This will make for easy replacement when you have completed your Alaskan adventure.

Fifth wheels should be protected in a similar fashion, on the lower front portion of the rig. It is not necessary to put plywood on the upper front portion, however, a rock guard on the front window is necessary. If the fifth wheel has front power jacks, be sure all lead-ins and switches are protected.

Internal RV Care. Plan to travel light, not as though you were traveling to Florida in the winter. Extra weight adds up to trouble in the form of hotter tires, more strain on springs and suspension as well as more heat on bearings.

Pack breakable dishes with foam or tissues between each piece. This reduces noise, rattling, and eventual breakage. Remove knick-knacks from shelves. Limit canned goods. Do not plan to cook with a microwave oven unless your generator can run it. Even in private campgrounds with electric hookups there is not enough power to operate microwaves, air conditioners, heat strips, or fifteen-hundred-watt portable heaters.

Your rig will get a lot of jostling in construction areas. Cabinets should lock securely and the drawer that does not close tight will come out and spill. If you have ever removed your stove or refrigerator, check to make sure each is properly reinstalled. Frig-lock door lock is recommended for your refrigerator door regardless of what type is already on your unit.

Spare Parts. The following items should properly prepare you for your Alaska-Yukon travels. Make sure that the spare part you bring is the right size for your needs, and that it works.

- ☐ Spare tire and rim for each vehicle
- ☐ Water pump for potable system
- ☐ Complete set of fuses for your RV
- ☐ Wheel bearing, set for each rig
- ☐ 2 10-foot sewer hoses and coupler
- ☐ 1 Y water hose connector
- ☐ Siphoning hose
- ☐ Points, condenser, spark plugs
- ☐ Lawn chair for each traveler
- ☐ Air pressure gauge
- ☐ Vehicle air filter

- ☐ Catch-all box containing such items as plastic tape, wire, strong all-purpose glue, selection of screws, rubber washers, matches, candles, and other doodads.
- ☐ Extra set of belts
- ☐ Thermostat for engine
- ☐ 25-foot water hose
- ☐ 25-foot extension cord
- ☐ 2 large rolls of duct tape
- ☐ Jumper cables
- ☐ Tool kit

For caravans, Dave Stevens's checklist is all-sufficient. Since, however, you will not be traveling in the company of a "wagonmaster" whose rig would often contain some additional items, we suggest you add the following.

- ☐ First-aid kit
- ☐ Tow cable (about 20 feet)
- ☐ Flashlight and spare batteries
- ☐ Multipurpose dry chemical fire extinguisher
- ☐ Ax or hatchet (if you want to use cut but unsplit logs at most government campsites)

- ☐ Small mop and water bucket, for washing down your RV's exterior at lake or streamside
- ☐ Pocketknife
- ☐ Flare and reflectors

You might want to bring along your winter snow chains. No, you will not run into snow and ice if you come in the warm weather seasons; as a matter of fact the chances are pretty substantial that even if you bring chains you will never use them. Still, two friends of ours recently found theirs was the only vehicle in a long line of RVs and cars that did not slide off an unbelievably slick portion of wet detour road between Whitehorse and Haines Junction. Their secret: the set of chains he put on their rig when they saw the problem they were facing.

Preparing Your Automobile

Perhaps you have seen pictures of automobiles rigged for travel on the Alaska Highway and other North Country roads during the late 1940s and early 1950s. The vehicles, to our eyes today, appear almost comical. Several extra spare tires are loaded on top and at the rear of each car, as well as containers of emergency supplies and equipment. Extra cans of gasoline are precariously attached to rear bumpers. Frequently a hand-scrawled sign proclaims, "Alaska or Bust!"

Alas, many of them burst.

These days, if you are going to utilize your family automobile either to carry a tent or pull a trailer, preparing the vehicle for the rigors of the north is much simpler, because Northland travel is much less rigorous than it used to be.

Unless you plan to undertake one or more of the really remote highways (such as the Dempster into Canada's Northwest Territories), it is not necessary to carry extra fuel tanks or more than one spare tire. The tires and spare you do have on your vehicle, however, should be in first-rate condition. In fact, your whole car should be well tuned and operating at top efficiency. The "last frontier" is no place to be caught with a cylinder on the sick list or points not in synch.

In the way of special equipment, the headlight protectors and front-end screens recommended for RVs are just as appropriate for cars and station wagons as they are for camper trucks and motorhomes. Since automobiles do not have the assortment of valves, copper pipes, and outlets that motorhomes and travel trailers often have on their underbellies, no special deflectors nor special covers are needed in this area.

We recommend that you carry the following spare parts and supplies: fuses, points, spark plugs, fan belt, trailer bearing (if you are pulling a trailer), jumper cables, well-stocked tool kit, first-aid kit, pocket knife, flashlight and spare batteries, flare and reflectors, ax or hatchet, lug wrench, and car jack.

If you do develop a problem, North Country shops, even out in the boonies, are reasonably well stocked, and the ability of innovative northern mechanics to "make do" is legendary. If, however, your car is a rare breed of foreign manufacture, you should probably consult with your local dealer for a list of additional parts to bring along.

Preparing Your Motorbike

You do not see a great number of motorbikes along northern highways nor in northern campgrounds, but if this is your way of travel there is certainly no reason to forgo a motorbike-tenting vacation in Alaska and Canada's Yukon.

There is not a lot of extra preparation necessary to put a bike in shape for travel in the north. The service department people at Honda Hut in Juneau did advise us that wrapping and securing foam around the front forks could aid in keeping rocks and gravel from working into the steering and shock mechanisms. It would, as well, protect the motorbike's finish. They recommend making sure your motorbike is well tuned and has good tires before ever undertaking the trip. A high-impact windscreen is definitely called for.

In the way of spare parts, they recommend carrying extra points, spark plugs and other tune-up parts, a spare headlight, and an oil filter.

Preparing Your Bicycle

Most of the bicycles you see in Alaskan and Yukon campgrounds get there on the front or back of an RV. They are handy for short trips to the store or for close-to-camp exploring. Many others arrive in the cargo compartments of jets. But a number of hardy two-wheel trippers do pedal north each year from the lower forty-eight states and provinces utilizing the Alaska state ferries in southeastern Alaska (bikes travel free) and the highways of the state and territory elsewhere.

All of Alaska's major cities have well-equipped bicycle sales and repair shops. Outside of the main urban areas, however, the biker is pretty much on his or her own when it comes to replacement parts or repair.

Therefore it is extremely important to carry a well-stocked extra-parts bag, even though the extra ounces do add up to pounds. Here, in addition to camping gear, is what you should bring along: two extra tubes, one extra tire, tube repair kit, tire pump, extra cable for each brake, extra cable for each gear shifter, extra spokes, extra brake pads, and a well-equipped tool kit with a wrench (including Allen wrench) to fit every nut and bolt on your bike. Because you will be cycling in wet weather or on wet roads at least part of the time, we highly recommend fenders both fore and aft.

If you are selecting a bike just for this trip, we suggest you strongly consider a lightweight mountain bike. The fat tires are much more compatible with the occasional gravel you will encounter on some highways, in construction areas, and in campgrounds. (If yours is a standard ten-speed bike however, do not let this suggestion scare you; we have pedaled throughout southeastern Alaska, southcentral, and the Interior on this kind of equipment, and we have gotten along fine.)

Bicycle camping in Alaska is tremendous fun, but it does require both long- and short-range planning. Always carry along at least a one- or two-day supply of food. You may or (more frequently) may not be within pedaling distance of a grocery store or restaurant at meal times.

A final note on equipment: for protection against rain, line the inside of your bags and panniers with plastic sacks. Bring lightweight rain gear (bike ponchos are fine but you will need rain pants as well) plus layers of T-shirts, warm shirts, sweater, down or Thinsulate vest, windbreaker, shorts, long trousers, and wool socks. (Yes, it can be very warm in Alaska in the summer, but there are cold, wet days as well. Prepare for them.)

When to Travel

Camping and trailering in Alaska and the Yukon is for late spring, summer, and early fall. June through August are the peak months and the warmest ones. Everything in the way of visitor sights, services, and tours is open and going full tilt. The last half of May and the first three weeks or so of September offer almost as many visitor opportunities; and in many places and instances, the cost of tours and attractions may be somewhat lower.

Depending on the region it can be somewhat colder in May and wetter in September than during the main tourist season. But on the roads and in the campgrounds the crowds and clutter are noticeably less. The first snow often hits around the first of October.

Travel Options

The Alaska Highway. Many people, when they think of motoring to Alaska, think in terms of round-trip travel via the Alaska Highway. That is certainly a viable, exciting option; but it is only one of several routes you can travel.

The Alaska Marine Highway. From the ports of Seattle, Washington; Prince Rupert, British Columbia; and tiny Hyder, Alaska, the state of Alaska operates a frequent schedule of oceangoing passenger and vehicle ferries. These are modern, roomy, comfortable vessels, and they connect the other states of the United States and Canada with the principal towns and villages of southeastern Alaska. From Haines or Skagway at the northern end of the ferry route you can drive mostly paved highways through British Columbia and the Yukon on into the rest of Alaska.

British Columbia Ferries. Another ferry option is the British Columbia Ferries vessel MV *Queen of the North*, which connects Port Hardy on Vancouver Island with the Alaska ferries at Prince Rupert, British Columbia.

Combined Road-Ferry. You can combine Alaska Highway, Alaska Marine Highway and/or British Columbia ferries segments, and make your trip a driving vacation one direction, ferry the other.

Cruise Ship Travel. Interestingly, luxury cruising is now an option for the vacationing motorist. Since 1985, Admiral Cruises (1220 Biscayne Boulevard, Miami, Florida 33101) has operated its elegant MS *Stardancer* from Vancouver, British Columbia, to and through the Alaska panhandle to Haines and Skagway. This deluxe vessel carries not only passengers but autos and RVs as well. At either of the two northernmost cities of the panhandle, you can drive off and continue the balance of your visit by road. In the meantime you have enjoyed the good life of cruise ship sailing, which includes first-class staterooms, delicious dining, theater, gym, swimming, casino, and all the other benefits of shipboard accommodations.

Following are current sample fares, travel times, and mileages. Vehicle charges are based on length of vehicle. Staterooms are available with two, three, and four berths. Bear in mind that these prices are subject to change.

From	Passenger	24′ RV	15′–19′ car	2-berth cabin	hours/miles

Fares on the Alaska Marine Highway System:

From	Passenger	24′ RV	15′–19′ car	2-berth cabin	hours/miles
Seattle-Skagway	$208	$1050	$624	$171	60/1090
Prince Rupert-Ketchikan	$ 24	$ 114	$ 70	$ 31	6/103
Ketchikan-Juneau	$ 62	$ 304	$182	$ 56	18/250
Juneau-Haines	$ 18	$ 84	$ 52	$ 28	6.5/77

Fares on British Columbia Ferries (Canadian currency):

From	Passenger	24′ RV	15′–19′ car	2-berth cabin	hours/miles
Port Hardy-Prince Rupert	$ 50	$193.50		day trip	15/274

Fares on the cruise ship *Stardancer:*

From	Passenger	24′ RV	15′–19′ car	2-berth cabin	hours/miles
Vancouver-Skagway	$660	$480		included	4 days cruising

RV Caravans. Several companies offer caravan tours to Alaska. Your only obligation, in addition to paying a fee, is simply to show up with your RV at a designated rendezvous point and join with a dozen to two dozen other travelers for several weeks of pleasurable preplanned touring.

For the traveler who wants to enjoy the countryside yet leave planning, logistics, sightseeing tours, shows, some meals, and lots of other details to the experts, this is a great way to travel. The only Alaska company offering this service at present is Alaska-Yukon RV Caravans, of Hyder. The firm's booking office is located at 10518 NE 37th Circle, Suite A, Kirkland, Washington 98033. The company offers all-land tours plus combination land-cruise ship itineraries.

Fly and Rent. If time is a factor you can fly to Alaska and the Yukon then rent an RV once you get here. Rentals are available in Anchorage, Soldotna, Fairbanks, Whitehorse, and Haines. Companies that rent them include: Number One Motorhome Rentals of Alaska, 322 Concrete Street, Anchorage, Alaska 99501 (rentals in Anchorage, Soldotna, and Haines), phone 907-277-7575; Alaska Panorama R.V. Rentals, 8215 East Second Avenue, Anchorage, Alaska 99504, phone 907-338-1401; Alaska RV Tours, 3002 Spenard Road, Anchorage, Alaska 99503, phone 907-274-2573; Clippership Motorhome Rentals, 3200 Mountainview Drive, Suite B, Anchorage, Alaska 99501, phone 907-276-6491; Go Vacations, Box 4-2440, Anchorage, Alaska 99509, phone 907-563-0013; Sourdough Camper Village, Box 100079, Anchorage, Alaska 99501, phone 907-563-3277; Sweet Retreat Motorhome Rentals, 3605 Arctic, #1047, Anchorage, Alaska 99503, phone 907-345-3889; Alaska Recreational Rentals, Box 2586, Soldotna, Alaska 99669, phone 907-262-1303; C & D Enterprises, 470 McKinley View Drive, Fairbanks, Alaska 99701, phone 907-457-4188; Van Alaska, Box 60091, Fairbanks, Alaska 99706, phone 907-456-1170.

In the Yukon, campers and motorhomes may be rented from Klondike Recreational Rentals, Ltd., Box 5156, Whitehorse, Yukon Territory, Canada Y1A 4S3, phone 403-668-2200.

United States Airlines Serving Alaska

If the Fly and Rent option interests you, you can fly to Alaska from the lower forty-eight states and Hawaii on the following airlines: Air Cal, Alaska Airlines, Hawaiian Airlines, Trans World Airlines (TWA), Northwest Orient, Reeve Aleutian Airways, South Pacific Airways, United Airlines, and Western Airlines.

Canadian Airlines Serving the Yukon Territory

If you want to rent an RV in Whitehorse, you can fly there via Canadian Pacific Airlines or Pacific Western. Yukon's Air North also provides scheduled service from Juneau.

Mileposts and Kilometerposts

They come in varied sizes, shapes and colors, but the handiest aid to travel in the North Country are the mileposts in Alaska and the kilometerposts in Canada, which you see every few miles (or kilometers) alongside the road. The numbers written on them represent miles or kilometers from the beginning of a highway. As a general rule (there are exceptions) the numbering runs south to north and east to west with mile 0 or kilometer 0 being the southernmost or easternmost end of the highway.

On the Richardson Highway out of Valdez, for instance, the number "85" would indicate you are 85 miles from the Valdez start of the road. If you are driving north, looking for the campground at Dry Creek State Recreation Site, which we list at Mile 117.5, you know that you have 32.5 miles yet to go. A similar post in the Yukon would indicate kilometers, not miles.

For the most part (again, with exceptions), in this book we have listed campgrounds along the highways south to north and east to west. If you are traveling a road in the reverse direction from which it is written, then you should turn to the end of the highway section and note the listings in reverse order.

Alaska's older mileposts are white horizontal signs with black lettering. On newer or recently reconstructed roads they are green with white lettering. In the Yukon the kilometerposts are white posts only, with no horizontal crossbars. The kilometer numbers are stenciled vertically on the post's sides.

And, we have to say it, a lot of the mile and kilometer addresses for government and private campgrounds, as well as businesses, lodges and even communities, can be confusing. In the Yukon in particular, brochures and even government guides will list a site or service at "kilometerpost such-and-such" and will show the equivalent "milepost such-and-such" in brackets. Which is great until you try converting the kilometers into miles and you find that the conversions in the brackets are off by a few miles. Other times the conversions are right on. It is no big deal, however. The numbers are never far enough off to cause a problem. We mention it only so you will not be surprised.

Miles and Metric Madness

United States citizens, unless they are used to metric standards, may at first be confused by the Canadian way of measuring: kilometers instead of miles, meters instead of yards and feet, liters instead of quarts and gallons. All we can say is, relax, you will get used to it in no time.

Here are some metric equivalents which, if you are like us, you will forget before you get past the next page. A kilometer is roughly six-tenths of a mile. A mile is roughly one and six-tenths kilometers.

Here is an easy way to convert one to the other. On most newer cars and RVs, manufacturers show both miles per hour and kilometers per hour on the speedometer. Frequently the miles per hour will be printed just above the kilometers per hour, usually in a different color. By looking at your speedometer you can see that fifty-five miles per hour, for example, is pretty close to ninety kilometers per hour. Thus you know that ninety kilometers is about the same as fifty-five miles. Another example: If you are looking for a campground that is thirty kilometers down the road, look at your speedometer and you will see that thirty kilometers per hour is approximately eighteen miles per hour. Now you know you have about eighteen miles to go.

While in Canada, we suggest you forget about making conversions and simply *think metric*. It will take a few hours, maybe even a day or two, but soon it will not matter how many miles it is from place to place. The scenery is every bit as exciting whether measured in miles or kilometers.

When you gas up, remember that the station attendant will measure your tankful in liters, not gallons. A liter is just short of a United States quart. A Canadian gallon (4.6 liters) is one-fifth larger than a United States gallon. Again, our suggestion is not to concern yourself with making conversion. Your primary concern, most of the time, should be simply to make sure your tank has plenty of fuel to make it to the next stop. Try always to have at least a half a tank of gasoline in your tank. When you drop near the half-full mark, it is time to fuel up.

Time Zones

Telling the time used to be confusing in the North Country; Alaska alone had four different zones. But no more. Most of Alaska (except western Alaska and the Aleutian Islands) is now on Alaska time, which is one hour earlier than Pacific time on which the United States west coast, British Columbia, and the Yukon operate. Thus, when it is 1:00 P.M. in Seattle and Whitehorse, it is noon in Juneau and Anchorage, and 11:00 A.M. along the Aleutian chain.

Crossing the Border

Border procedure, whether crossing into or out of Canada or the United States, is a cinch. No passports or visas are required, though you should have some identification to indicate your place of residence and citizenship. You may be asked to show a child's birth certificate.

The Canada customs people may ask you to show that you have enough money, travelers checks, or credit cards to make it through their country.

You are *not* allowed to transport handguns through Canada.

You may be asked to show proof of insurance coverage. The easiest way to do this is to obtain a Canadian Nonresident Interprovince Motor Vehicle Liability Card from your insurance agent. These cards are available only in the United States through United States insurance agents. Minimum liability coverage for travel in the Yukon Territory is $200,000.

Americans returning to the United States can bring in Canadian goods worth up to $400 (United States currency) without paying duty on the merchandise. You can also bring in one liter of liquor duty free, if you are twenty-one or older.

You can bring your pet with you into Canada and the United States provided you have a valid, current rabies vaccination certificate for the animal.

Bears and Mosquitoes

It is difficult to determine which it is that potential travelers are more apprehensive about—bears or mosquitoes. Some years ago, we represented the state of Alaska at travel and outdoor shows all over the United States and the most frequent questions we answered had to do with the carnivorous nature of both these creatures.

First, about mosquitoes. They are there. You will see them, swat them, and curse them. It seems to us they are no worse in Alaska than we have experienced in many other locales in the United States and Canada. Dowse yourself with bug repellent if you are heading into the deep woods, or if a particularly large gathering of these determined insects has located your campsite. We like Cutters and Muskol. Long pants and a long-sleeved shirt will do a lot to discourage them. A few overly zealous folks even bring head nets! You should, however, make sure that the screens on all your RV windows are intact.

Bear danger is similarly overrated. But, let us add that if you do come into contact with a black, brown, or grizzly bear, do not minimize the possible danger from these kings of the Alaska forest and tundra. Do not approach them. Telephoto, not close-up, are the lens options of choice when taking their pictures. If you are tent camping, be sure to hang your food (including candy and toothpaste) well away from your campsite and anyone else's. If a bear does invite himself to your dinner table outdoors, be a gracious host and let him take all he wants—which will probably be your entire meal. (The chances of this happening are remote, but at Byer's Lake Campground along the Parks Highway a few years back a certain grizzly arrived at the picnic area promptly at dinnertime each evening for several weeks. At long last, park rangers succeeded in trapping him and transporting him far from the site of his easy pickings.)

What to Wear

The proper wardrobe for an Alaska-Yukon visit is emphatically casual. If you like an occasional formal night on the town, bring one dressy outfit for the lady and one coat and tie outfit for the man—perhaps for a special dinner at the likes of Josephine's in Anchorage. The rest of your wardrobe should be comfortable and practical.

Wash-and-wear pants, blue jeans, flannel shirts, light wool sweaters, comfortable walking shoes ... these are the clothes you will wear during a vacation in the north. Important: Bring along a warm jacket for wear during frequently cool evenings and sometimes cold days. It need not be a heavy winter jacket. Instead, layer your clothes, adding wool shirts, sweaters, and jacket as it gets cooler, and take off layers when it warms up. Bring a raincoat for the inevitable showers that will fall during your stay. A pair of waterproof boots or shoes will likewise come in handy if you have to walk from your vehicle to a campground toilet over wet or muddy terrain.

Camping Fees

The biggest vacation bargain in Alaska is camping. The Alaska State Parks campgrounds, most of which we consider extraordinarily nice sites, are free at this time, (although the legislature may authorize fees in future years). So are waysides operated by the United States Bureau of Land Management and the United States Fish and Wildlife Service. (At one USFWS site, Kenai Russian River Campground, there is a charge.) The USFS usually charges five dollars to overnight in their facilities. The National Park Service campgrounds in Denali National Park and Preserve vary from free to eight dollars, depending on services available at each site. In Canada there is a five-dollar nightly nonresident fee for campgrounds run by the Yukon government, the Northwest Territories government, and Parks Canada. (Bargain hunters please note: Five dollars in Canadian currency equals about four dollars in United States currency. If you are going to camp in Yukon government campgrounds five nights or more you will be dollars ahead if you buy a twenty-five-dollar season camping permit.) Throughout this book, if there is a nightly charge at a public campground we show it, along with camping limits.

Churches

Travelers need never miss worship while traveling in Alaska and the Yukon. Roman Catholic, Orthodox Christian, and a variety of Protestant congregations are located in and near communities throughout the state and territory. Resident members take considerable pleasure in welcoming visitors to their services.

Fishing

It is no secret that sportfishing in Alaska and the Yukon ranks among the best in the world. Lunker king salmon, dancing rainbows, fighting lake trout, and many other species make northern waters a mecca for sport anglers. You will not find Alaska's best fishing at the roadside. That is where all the other fishermen are, so that is where the fish *used to be*. To partake of Alaska's and the Yukon's very best sportfishing you need to charter either a plane or a boat to take you away from the heavy pressure points. If that is not feasible, here is a technique that often proves successful. Park your vehicle near a bridge that crosses a likely stream, check your watch, and then hike for about a half hour either upstream or down before you put your line in the water. Your chances of hooking the evening's dinner is much greater than if you simply tried your luck near the bridge or a campground.

Fishing licenses in Alaska and the Yukon are available at government offices, sporting goods stores, highway lodges, and various other outlets. In Alaska the cost is thirty-six dollars for a nonresident annual license, twenty dollars for a fourteen-day permit, and ten dollars for three days.

In the Yukon a nonresident fishing permit costs twenty dollars for a year, ten dollars for five days, or five dollars for one day. Be aware of limits and regulations, all of which are set forth in free booklets available where you buy your license.

Money

The bad news is, things do tend to cost more in the North Country, and generally the farther north you go the higher the cost of food, fuel, and other items. The good news is, there are exceptions to the rule and big-city Anchorage is one of them. Prices are higher there than in Lower Forty-eight cities, but they are lower than most prices elsewhere in Alaska.

In many respects, Canadian travel sometimes approaches bargain status since the United States dollar is worth more than its Canadian equivalent. On our last trip north, Canadian banks were giving $1.35 in Canadian currency for $1.00 in United States money. Which brings up an important point: Exchange your money at Canadian banks. You will get a far better value—frequently ten cents or more to the dollar—than you would if you did your exchanging in a store.

Driving Distances and Times

Following are some sample distances and driving times in Alaska, the Yukon, and from the lower forty-eight states.

Seattle-Anchorage	7 days	2,435 miles
Seattle-Fairbanks	7 days	2,313 miles
Haines-Anchorage	17 hours	775 miles
Haines-Fairbanks	14 hours	653 miles
Skagway-Whitehorse	3 hours	108 miles
Skagway-Anchorage	20 hours	832 miles
Skagway-Fairbanks	17 hours	710 miles
Anchorage-Homer	5 hours	226 miles
Anchorage-Valdez	7 hours	304 miles
Fairbanks-Denali	2.5 hours	121 miles
Fairbanks-Valdez	7 hours	284 miles
Anchorage-Fairbanks (via Parks Highway)	7.5 hours	358 miles
Anchorage-Fairbanks (via Glenn Highway)	12 hours	404 miles

(Miles and estimated driving times provided by the Alaska Division of Tourism.)

Listings in This Book

In the following four chapters we list and describe every state, territorial, and federal campground in the state of Alaska and in Yukon Territory. We list, as well, every municipal and community facility we could uncover. Based on personal visits or on reports we trust from other campers, agencies, or parks officials, we attempt to give you an idea of what you will find at each location—good and bad features. Obviously, things change and today's mediocre campsite may become tomorrow's outstanding outdoor destination.

Your impressions of the various campgrounds you visit here are requested. Letting us know the strengths and weaknesses of the sites where you camp could make revisions of this book even more valuable, for future travelers, than this edition. If you are willing to do this, jot down your thoughts and send them to Mike and Marilyn Miller, P.O. Box 021494, Juneau, Alaska 99802.

Now, about private or commercial campgrounds. You will note that with very few exceptions we have not described them. We have, however, listed as many as we could locate. We have not gone into detail about them because the quality of many private campgrounds varies greatly from year to year—far more so than public campgrounds. This is probably due to changing ownership, changing economic conditions on the part of the owners, perhaps even around-the-clock, high-pressure "burnout" over the years.

More important, with some notable exceptions, we find most of the commercial campgrounds in the North Country to be pretty lackluster at best. We do recognize there are exceptions: The Sourdough Campground at Tok, for instance, is absolutely first rate. Its well-tended wooded grounds, services, and friendly operators make it a delightful choice for travelers who enjoy the advantages of commercial facilities. Both Alaska KOAs are similarly worthwhile. The private campground at Takhini Hot Springs near Whitehorse is absolutely terrific. There are others, of course.

But at many, many commercial campgrounds in the Northland what you will find is a cleared gravel lot, little if any separation between spaces, sometimes showers and sometimes not, and—at many locations—pieces of discarded heavy equipment lying within view of the camper.

In fairness we should point out that many, probably most, of the private operators do provide electric and water hookups, dump stations, and perhaps repair services, fuel, restaurant, or bar facilities. Some gas station owners will let you camp free on their premises (without hookups) if you fuel up at their facility.

Here are our thoughts about Alaska's and the Yukon's public campgrounds. They are not fancy, they are rustic, but they are decidedly for the most part clean, well maintained, and relatively uncrowded (except near large cities or special destination areas such as the best fishing holes on the Kenai Peninsula). There are seldom hookups or even dump stations but there are usually one or more water wells, toilets, tables, picnic facilities, fire grates, and cut firewood.

For the most part, camper spaces in the public campgrounds are separated by a screen of trees or plants. Frequently there are at least a few pull-through spaces for the convenience of large trailers.

All of the Yukon's campgrounds are situated near lakes, creeks, or rivers. Most of Alaska's are in this same category. Except near the large cities there is almost uniformly the feel of being in wondrously wild and unspoiled country. The sounds of night after you retire each evening are of rushing stream waters, or at lakeside of geese honking and loons trilling, or of gentle winds blowing through the trees.

Selecting Your Travel Route

Selecting your route to and within Alaska and the Yukon is not that difficult, because there are relatively few roads to and through the

Northland. Depending on where in the lower forty-eight states you start from there are convenient north-leading highways from Seattle, Wenatchee, and Spokane in Washington State; Coeur d'Alene, Idaho; and Missoula, Helena, and Great Falls, Montana. These and connecting highways lead toward Dawson Creek, British Columbia, where the Alaska Highway starts and to Prince Rupert, British Columbia, where the Alaska Marine Highway begins.

As noted earlier in this chapter, the ferry system winds through southeastern Alaska to its northern terminals at Skagway and Haines. From there you can drive the Klondike or Haines highways, respectively, and connect with the Alaska Highway at or just north of Whitehorse. If you can afford it we recommend a circle route, utilizing all-highway travel one direction and a ferry trip the other. Generally speaking, the ferry vessels are most crowded northbound from mid-June through July and southbound in late August.

Following are examples of other circle routes in the Northland.

Instead of driving the full length of the Alaska Highway twice between Whitehorse and the Alaska border, it is possible to make a loop from Whitehorse taking in Dawson City, Yukon Territory, then rejoining the Alaska Highway just inside the Alaska Border at Tetlin Junction. (For details, see page 74.)

Once inside the main body of Alaska, when you get to Tok you can keep on driving northwest to Fairbanks on the Alaska and Richardson highways, or you can head southwest on the Tok Cutoff/Glenn Highway route to Anchorage (we usually drive the latter route). When you get to Anchorage you can spin down to the Kenai Peninsula for a few days then return to Anchorage and head north on the Parks Highway to Denali National Park and Preserve and on to Fairbanks. When you get ready to leave you can then drive the Richardson and Alaska highways to Tok. If you want to reverse this routing and travel Tok-Fairbanks-Anchorage-Tok, that works just as well.

Depending on the time you have available, plan to drive at least one, and hopefully more than one, of Alaska's lesser highways: the Steese to Circle Hot Springs, the Elliott to Manley Hot Springs, the Taylor to historic Eagle, the Edgerton to Chitina, or the Hope Highway to the tiny little community of Hope.

Whatever your route, however much time you have, stop often as you drive to savor the glistening glaciers, the untamed rivers, the virgin forests, and the sky-piercing mountains. There is no other place like this on earth. Like many other visitors to the North Country, you will relive again and again the views and vistas of this magnificent parcel of God's creation.

Alaska's Panhandle and Southeast Highways to the Yukon Territory

U ntil the early sixties, southeastern Alaska was pretty much off limits to recreational vehicle travelers. Among southeastern Alaskans there were many who, if you had asked them, could not have told you what "RV" stood for.

It is not hard to imagine why. The region is quite unlike any other in the United States. Southeast is more than five hundred miles long and up to one hundred miles wide. The region is mostly a mass of more than one thousand big and little islands. The islands are bordered on the east by a roughly thirty-mile-wide sliver of United States mainland and on the west by the Pacific Ocean.

In the years prior to 1962, the region did not have traditional highways connecting the various towns of the area. Fact is, traditional interconnecting highways still do not exist here, and probably never will. But starting in 1962 a frequent schedule of fast, comfortable (some even say elegant) ferries began providing what Alaskans call the Marine Highway service to and through the panhandle.

What an absolutely dynamite way to get around!

Five major vessels provide service either from Seattle, Washington (twice a week in summer), or from Prince Rupert, British Columbia, Canada (almost daily), to Ketchikan, Wrangell, Petersburg, Sitka, Juneau, Haines, and Skagway in Alaska. That is the system's "mainline" service. Three smaller ships provide connecting service to smaller towns and villages throughout the Bush (sparsely populated, isolated area).

The ferries look a lot like luxury cruise ships (in spite of their nickname, the "blue canoes") and they boast staterooms, cocktail lounges, cafeteria dining accommodations, ample observation areas, and delightful heated top-deck solariums. The vessels can carry several hundred passengers and more than a hundred vehicles, including RVs. The smaller ferries have less passenger and vehicle capacity and do not have overnight accommodations, but they are otherwise every bit as comfortable. Many travelers enjoy them more because, even on a short trip, it seems easier to make friends with fellow travelers and with the locals.

"Driving" the Alaska Marine Highway is like no other road trip you are likely to undertake. At Seattle, or at Prince Rupert (or at Haines or Skagway if you are already in Alaska, and heading south), you simply drive your vehicle aboard, park where a crewman directs you in the spacious car deck, then walk upstairs to the passenger levels topside. (Elevator service is available on most vessels, if you need it.) Your stateroom, if you reserved one, is assigned by the ship's purser; after you have stowed your luggage you can begin a tour of the vessel.

Want to relax for a while? There are glassed-in observation lounges with comfortable chairs both fore and aft, port and starboard. In one of these areas, at designated times, uniformed naturalists of the USFS will lecture about the lands and waters you are cruising through.

Hungry? A cafeteria offers everything from snacks and sandwiches to fresh Alaska salmon and other seafood delicacies.

Thirsty? The ship's bar can serve up libations from light drinks and beer to Alaska Moose Milk, a smooth but deceptively devastating concoction of milk, eggs, sugar, and no small measure of hard liquors.

Tired? If you have not reserved a stateroom, you can snooze on reclining airline-type seats or (our choice) you can spread your sleeping bag on the top deck beneath a glass-enclosed solarium. You cannot, unfortunately, go below deck and sleep in your vehicle. The ferries used to permit this, but unfortunately a few thoughtless individuals persisted in breaking the rules by lighting cook stoves—potentially a most explosive situation.

The miles cruise gently by as the captain and his crew navigate between islands of thick, lush rain forests. Mountains rise dramatically from the sea to cloud-hidden heights. On other peaks, the white snow and ice patches of hanging glaciers cling between the sloping surfaces of granite crags and even on the faces of sheer cliffs. Waterfalls cascade into the ocean currents. And eagles. Everywhere there are eagles, but you never tire of watching their powerful, tireless flight.

The captain occasionally may announce the presence of killer or humpback whales, or porpoises alongside the ship. When that happens there is an elbow-to-elbow rush to deck-rail vantage points to see and photograph these living wonders of the sea.

Perhaps the grandest feature of traveling the Marine Highway is the flexibility it affords. You can disembark with your vehicle at one, or all, of your vessel's ports of call. Stay a day, a week, or even longer, then catch another ferry at your convenience and continue your voyage.

At the end of the ferry route you are back on land again and your adventure continues. Could anything be more pleasant?

Traveling by cruise ship will offer about the same itinerary. In recent years Sundance Cruises' MS *Stardancer*—a truly luxurious vessel with swimming pool, disco, casino, health club, deluxe staterooms and public

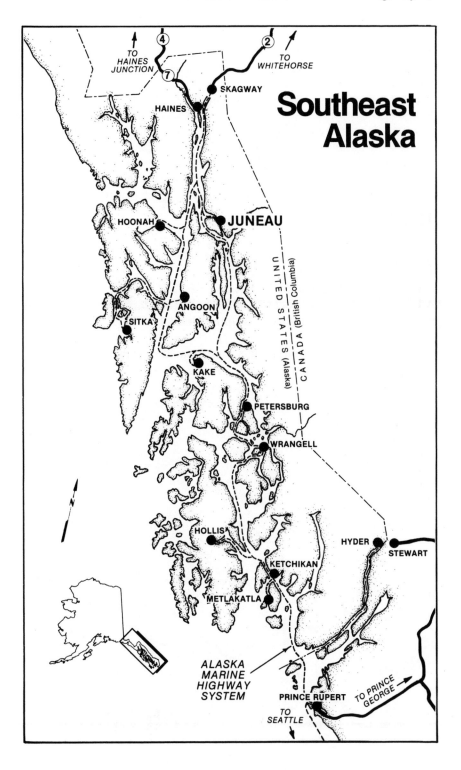

Southeast Alaska

TO
HAINES
JUNCTION

4

7

2

TO
WHITEHORSE

SKAGWAY

HAINES

HOONAH

JUNEAU

UNITED STATES (Alaska)

CANADA (British Columbia)

ANGOON

SITKA

KAKE

PETERSBURG

WRANGELL

HOLLIS

HYDER

STEWART

KETCHIKAN

METLAKATLA

ALASKA
MARINE
HIGHWAY
SYSTEM

PRINCE RUPERT

TO PRINCE
GEORGE

TO
SEATTLE

rooms plus capacity for cars and RVs—has operated from Vancouver, British Columbia, through the Southeast panhandle. There is not quite the same degree of drive-on, drive-off flexibility you have with the state ferries; you can not take your vehicle off the ship until it arrives in either Haines or Skagway (or, heading south, until it reaches Vancouver), but the service and accommodations are deliciously first class.

Following are campgrounds located along the routes of the major vessels of the Southeast Marine Highway system. For campground locations along the Bush routes served by smaller ferries, see pages 52–56.

Ketchikan

SIGNAL CREEK CAMPGROUND (USFS)
THREE C'S CAMPGROUND (USFS)
LAST CHANCE CAMPGROUND (USFS)
All three campgrounds located on Ward Creek Road, which junctions with North Tongass Highway at approximately Mile 7.

All three of these campgrounds are located near the shores of Ward

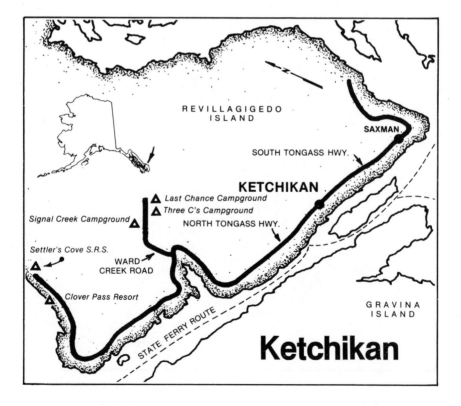

Lake; a particularly scenic body of water surrounded by a forest of huge spruce and hemlock trees. Anglers who fish in the lake or in Ward Creek have fair luck catching cutthroat trout, Dolly Varden, rainbow trout, silver salmon, pink salmon, and steelhead trout. There are trails in the vicinity, and from the lake or along the trails you may see beavers, land otters, deer, black bears, eagles, and various other bird life.

Developed drinking water, toilets, and picnic facilities are located at each campground. Signal Creek, with 25 units, is located at Mile .7 on Ward Lake Road. Three C's, with 4 camping spaces, is at Mile 1. Last Chance, containing 23 units, is at Mile 3. There is a $5 daily fee and a 14-day camping limit at each.

CLOVER PASS RESORT (private)
Located at the end of half-mile North Point Higgins Road, which junctions with North Tongass Highway at Mile 14.

SETTLER'S COVE STATE RECREATION SITE (Alaska State Parks)
Mile 18.2 North Tongass Highway

Situated on the saltwater shores of Behm Canal, about a half-hour's drive northerly from Ketchikan, this campground contains 10 spaces for tenters and RVs. Water for drinking, handicap-access toilets, and picnic facilities are all on-site. If you can take the chilly waters, there is a pleasant gravel swimming beach. (Tip: Do your dipping on an incoming tide. The water temperature rises somewhat as it comes in over a warm beach.) There also is saltwater fishing from boats for salmon, halibut, and other species. The seascape view is marvelous. No fee; 15-day camping limit.

Wrangell

CITY PARK (city of Wrangell)
Mile 1.9 Zimovia Highway

This is a relatively small campground located next to a city ball park. Shelter and picnic facilities are nearby, as are flush toilets. Dump station is located downtown at Case Avenue and Front Street. Camping limit here is 2 days.

SHOEMAKER BAY (city of Wrangell)
Mile 4.7 Zimovia Highway

Located at Shoemaker Bay small-boat harbor, this city-operated facility offers camping accommodations for both tenters and RVs as well as

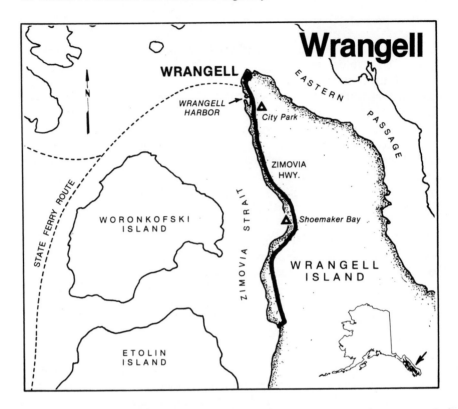

hookups, picnic facilities, dump station, toilets, even a tennis court and playground. A mile-long trail to Rainbow Falls takes off from here.

Petersburg

"TENT CITY" CAMPGROUND (city of Petersburg)
Located on Haugen Drive.

This facility is unique in Alaska—a tenters' campground on raised wooden platforms complete with drinking water, cooking area, and rest rooms. RVs can park here as well. The site is, however, frequently full during the summer when cannery workers come to town. Fee is $3 a day; $20 a week with a refundable $25 deposit.

SOUTH HARBOR STAGING AREA (city of Petersburg)
One-half mile north of ferry terminal.

RVs may park/camp in this area for 8 hours. No fee; no permit required.

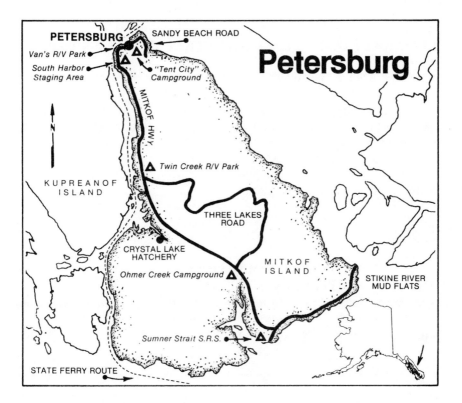

VAN'S R/V PARK (private)
Located at 4th and Haugen streets.

TWIN CREEK R.V. PARK (private)
Located at Mile 7.5 Mitkof Highway.

OHMER CREEK CAMPGROUND (USFS)
Mile 22 Mitkof Highway

Fifteen travel trailers, motorhomes, campers, or tents can be accommodated in this campground about 21 miles south of the ferry landing. Grills, tables, toilets, and drinking water are on-site. Fishing is considered good for Dolly Varden, cutthroat trout, and silver salmon. Black bears and Sitka blacktailed deer are common on Mitkof Island where Petersburg is located. You may see them while hiking in the area. The USFS requests that campers please haul out their own trash. There is a 14-day camping limit.

SUMNER STRAIT STATE RECREATION SITE (Alaska State Parks)
Mile 26.8 Mitkof Highway

This campground is described as "unmaintained," which means there are no developed facilities such as water, toilets, picnic tables, or trash barrels. (What you haul in, please haul out.) There is, however, plenty of room for parking/camping. No less than six species of fish are reported to be available: king, silver, red, and pink salmon; Dolly Varden; and cutthroat trout. No fee; 15-day camping limit.

Sitka

STARRIGAVAN CAMPGROUND (USFS)
Mile 7.8 Halibut Point Road

Conveniently located just .7 mile from the ferry terminal, this campground seems like two; one part is on the ocean side of the paved

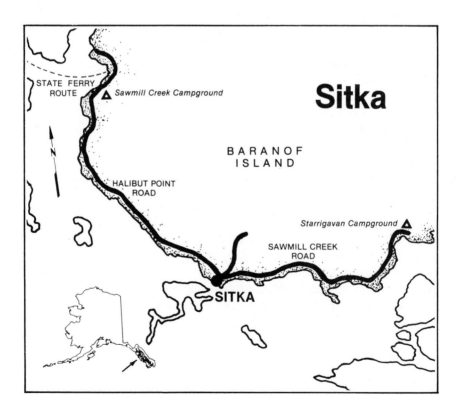

highway while the other part is upland from the road. Twenty-six camping units are maintained here along with toilets, fireplaces, and picnic tables. There is no developed water source. Creek water is available, but should be boiled or treated. Overnight spaces are scattered throughout the forest adjacent to a saltwater beach, an estuary, and a river. Dominated by water, woods, and mountains, the area provides a classic view of Mount Edgecumbe, a massive dormant volcano, which wins first prize in the Fujiyama-lookalike competition. No fee; no camping limit.

SAWMILL CREEK CAMPGROUND (USFS)
Mile 1.5 Blue Lake Road, which junctions with Sawmill Creek Road at Mile 5.4

Located 6 miles east of Sitka, this now-unmaintained wayside has 7 camping units, fireplaces, and toilets, but no water well. Creek water should be boiled or treated. If you are pulling much of a load you should look this road over before attempting its considerable climb. From the campground, situated on a large mountain creek closely surrounded by rugged mountains, you can sometimes see mountain goats on the heights north of the lake. Fishing in the area is for Dolly Varden, rainbow trout, and steelhead. Beaver Lake trail begins at the campground and heads for .8 mile up switchbacks and boardwalks on muskeg to Blue Lake. Since this campground is no longer maintained by the USFS it would be prudent to inquire at the USFS or city information offices about current conditions at the site. No fee; no camping limit.

Juneau

Here is some good news for Juneau visitors: Be aware that the city and borough (county) of Juneau issues "visitors extended time parking permits," which allow travelers to exceed the posted time limit on downtown parking spaces. These are available from the police department, downtown.

YACHT CLUB (city of Juneau)
Aurora Basin Small-Boat Harbor, Mile 1.7 Egan Expressway

This is not actually a campground but the city allows self-contained RVs to overnight on a paved parking area overlooking one of the municipality's small-boat harbors. Drinking water and toilet facilities are on-site. The area is only 5 minutes from the city center, state museum, Alaska's capitol building, and downtown shopping. Daily fee is $5; 7-day camping limit.

SUBPORT PARKING AREA (city of Juneau)
Mile .5 Egan Expressway

This is a paved parking area for Juneau downtown state workers and shoppers. RVs can overnight here at no charge. There is no view, but it is convenient to downtown, the state museum, and other state capitol buildings.

SHOPRITE MARKET (private)
Located at 1102 3rd Street, Douglas, approximately 2 miles south of the main bridge on Douglas Highway.

TIDES MOTEL AND CAMPER PARK (private)
Located at 5000 Glacier Highway.

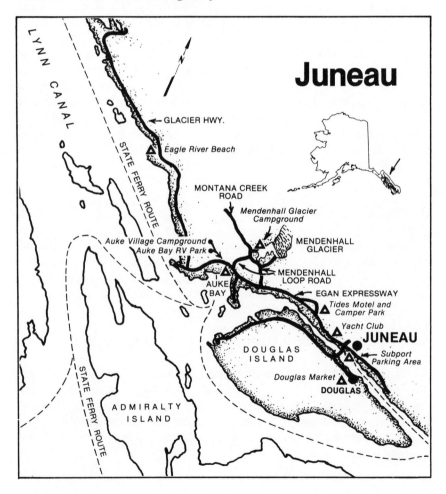

MENDENHALL GLACIER CAMPGROUND (USFS)
Mile .5 on Montana Loop Road, which junctions with Mendenhall Loop Road at Mile 3.7. (Mendenhall Loop Road, in turn, is accessed from junction at Mile 9 Egan Expressway).

This campground is what most travelers probably envision when they plan a trip to Alaska: Quiet, secluded woods-enclosed turnouts; an iceberg-studded lake setting; snowcapped mountains all around; and, dominating everything, across the lake a massive great blue glacier winding 12 miles downvalley from its source at a mountaintop icefield.

Sixty-one camping parties can be accommodated here. Ten units are for trailers up to 22 feet. Seven spaces are especially for backpackers. Tables, fireplaces, wood, water, toilets, and a central dump station are located on the grounds. Good hiking trails are located in the area, including our favorite in all Alaska—the West Glacier Trail beside and eventually overlooking Mendenhall Glacier. About 1.5 miles away, at the Mendenhall Glacier USFS Information Center, uniformed naturalists provide fascinating programs concerning the comings and goings of Alaska's rivers of ice. Daily fee is $5; 14-day camping limit.

AUKE BAY RV PARK (private)
Located at 11930 Glacier Highway.

AUKE VILLAGE CAMPGROUND (USFS)
Mile 15.4 Glacier Highway

Located 2 miles northwest (to the left) as you leave the Auke Bay ferry terminal, this campground offers 11 camping units, shelters, wood, water, toilets, and a forest setting beside one of the nicest gravel beaches in southeastern Alaska. The view is of water and wooded islands. Adjacent to the campground is a gravel swimming beach (for the hardy). The waters of the area abound with king and silver salmon. Daily fee is $5; 14-day camping limit.

EAGLE RIVER BEACH (USFS)
Mile 28 Glacier Highway

This is really a day-use area, and overnighters are not permitted in the section where picnic facilities are located. South of this section and just south of the Eagle River bridge, however, is a gravel area where self-contained RVs are occasionally allowed to park/camp. (See the USFS ranger at the Mendenhall Glacier Visitors Center.) Be aware, by the way, that noisy motorbikes and ATVs use this area. You might not get much sleep until late in the evening.

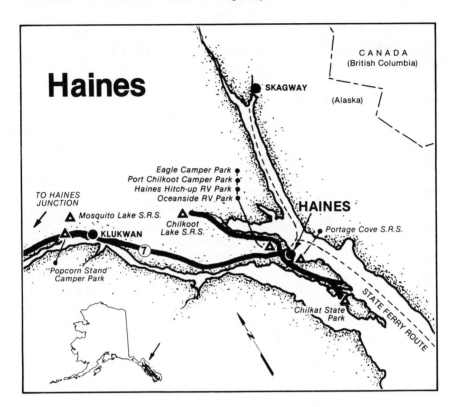

Haines

EAGLE CAMPER PARK (private)
Located on Union Street, in town.

PORT CHILKOOT CAMPER PARK (private)
Behind Halsingland Hotel in Port Chilkoot section of town.

HAINES HITCH-UP RV PARK (private)
At Y in road at entrance to town arriving from Canada.

OCEANSIDE RV PARK (private)
Located on Front Street.

PORTAGE COVE STATE RECREATION SITE (Alaska State Parks)
Located 2 miles from downtown Haines on Beach Road.

Backpackers and bicycle campers, this campground is for you—and only for you. No motorized vehicles are allowed. Accessible by a paved bike path, this tents-only facility offers 9 camping spaces, toilets, drinking water, and a terrific view of the fabulous Lynn Canal fjord. Dolly Varden are caught here, in addition to an occasional salmon. No fee; the 7-day camping limit is enforced.

CHILKAT STATE PARK (Alaska State Parks)
Mile 7 Mud Bay Road

This is one of the small treasures of the Alaska State Parks system. Unfortunately, when many northbound travelers disembark from the ferry they rush on to the Yukon without staying to savor this pleasurable Southeast parkland. Within its lush, timbered bounds are saltwater beaches, hiking trails, calendar-quality views of Davidson and Rainbow glaciers, ample fishing opportunities for salmon and Dolly Varden, perhaps a glimpse of a bear or moose, and definitely the sight of eagles.

A total of 33 developed camper spaces (some of them pull-throughs) plus numerous places for tenters are available in the park, as are handicap-access toilet facilities, drinking water, boat launch, picnic tables, and fireplaces. Be aware, however, there is a 1.5-mile, 11 percent grade on the road leading into the park. This steep an incline, plus washboarding that sometimes exists, could make pulling a big travel trailer a problem. No fee; there is a 7-day limit.

CHILKOOT LAKE STATE RECREATION SITE (Alaska State Parks)
Mile 10 Lutak Road

Here is another majestically situated campground, located on the shores of fish-filled Chilkoot Lake where it empties into the Chilkoot River. Rugged, snowcapped mountains surround the site, which also boasts a thick stand of sky-reaching spruce and hemlock.

Canoeing and boating are popular here, as are swimming and fishing for sockeye, pink, chum, and silver salmon. Brown bears are known to be in the general vicinity, though seldom if ever in the campground. If you see one, do not under any circumstances try to get near it, feed it, or in any way attract it. You may spot mountain goats on the mountainsides. Thirty-two camping units are located here along with handicap-access toilets, picnic accommodations, well water, and boat ramp. No fee; 7-day camping limit.

TEN MILE LODGE AND CAMPER PARK (private)
Mile 10 Haines Highway

MOSQUITO LAKE STATE RECREATION SITE (Alaska State Parks)
Access road at Mile 27 Haines Highway.

Do not let the name scare you. This campground—the last public wayside on the Alaska side of the border if you are heading north to Canada, and the first if you are coming south—harbors no more mosquitoes than any other. Nine camping units are located here, along with toilets, spring water, picnic shelter and facilities, a boat ramp, and a boat dock.

If you carry a canoe or boat, visit the far end of the lake. It is much prettier than the area near the campground. Fishing in the lake produces Dolly Varden, cutthroat, sockeye and silver salmon. You may see bears or mountain goats in the area.

Caution: This campground is off the highway and accessible by a 2.7-mile road. A pretty steep driveway with a rather sharp bend at the end could be troublesome for a big travel trailer. No fee; 7-day camping limit.

"POPCORN STAND" CAMPER PARK (private)
Mile 27 Haines Highway

Skagway

HANOUSEK PARK (city of Skagway)
Broadway and 14th Street

Located within the city in a timbered park, this wayside offers a dozen or so camping spaces on a first-come, first-served basis. Drinking water, pit toilets, hot showers, fire rings, and a dump station are on-site. Daily fee is $7.50 with electric hookups (4 sites only), $5.00 without; 5-day camping limit.

PULLEN CREEK PARK CAMPGROUND (city of Skagway)
Located on waterfront by a small-boat harbor.

Thirty-three sites are located here, with water, toilets, electric hookups, dump station, and showers. No open fires are allowed in this area. Daily fee is $10.50 with electric hookups, $8.00 without.

HOOVER'S CAMPGROUND (private)
Located at 4th and Main Street.

LIARSVILLE (state land)
Approximately 1.5 miles from ferry terminal on the Skagway River.

This area used to be a developed camping area but is now closed and there are no facilities on the site. RVs, however, may park here. It is definitely

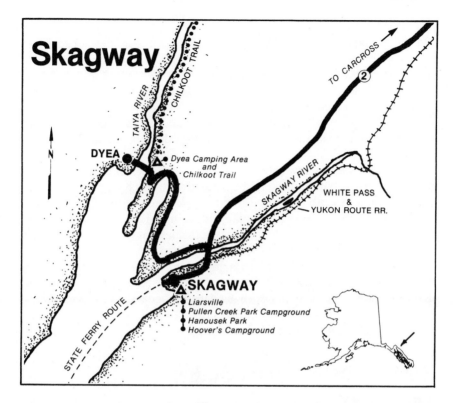

not a good choice, though, in times of heavy rains or rising river waters. During the era of the gold stampede back in the late 1890s, this was a historic camping locale for newly arrived prospectors. It got its name because of the caliber of the stories the local sourdoughs (old-timers) would tell the cheechakos (greenhorns or newcomers). Whatever you haul in, please haul out. No fee.

DYEA CAMPING AREA and CHILKOOT TRAIL (National Park Service)
Mile 6.7 Dyea Road

This is one of Alaska's most historic places and the trailhead of Alaska's most famous trek. Dyea was once a thriving community; now there is nothing left of the old town but a few relics. Around 1898, tens of thousands of gold stampeders set out from this site bound for the Klondike over the Chilkoot Trail. Today, that same path is an Alaska State Trail and is part of the Klondike Gold Rush National Historical Park, a unit of the National Park Service. A 22-unit National Park Service Campground is located at Dyea (pronounced Die-EEE), as is a National Park Service ranger station.

On-site are pit toilets, picnic tables, and fire rings but no developed water source. Caution: The road to Dyea is often rough, always curvy, and is not recommended for large RVs. No fee; 14-day limit.

The Chilkoot Trail itself is 33 miles long and is an international route under the jurisdiction of the United States National Park Service and Parks Canada. Roughly half the trail is in the United States, the other half in Canada. You can hike the trail in as few as three days, but taking four or five is more enjoyable.

Campsites and a few shelters are located on each side of the border. More than fifteen hundred hikers undertake the trek each year, most of them choosing to hike south to north as did the gold stampeders of '98.

Near the upper end of the trail, just north of Bare Loon lake, hikers head east to make access with the tracks of the now-inoperative White Pass and Yukon Route railroad. They then hike the tracks to Log Cabin on the Skagway-to-Whitehorse Klondike Highway. Except for a boring walk on the railroad right-of-way, the hike provides a marvelous blend of sea-level maritime forests; high-country open plateaus; plunging streams, placid lakes, hanging glaciers; and best of all, the historic, a-little-bit-scary, sometimes-cloud-covered, mountaintop Chilkoot Pass itself.

Bush Routes of the Southeast Marine Highway System

In addition to the four larger vessels of the Southeast ferry fleet, three smaller ferries provide service not only to major cities but also to small and isolated towns and villages. The vessels are the 235-foot MV *Aurora* (home port in Ketchikan), serving Prince Rupert, Hyder, and Hollis (on Prince of Wales Island); the 100-foot MV *Chilkat*, operating between Ketchikan and Metlakatla; and the 235-foot MV *LaConte*, connecting Petersburg, Kake, Sitka, Angoon, Tenakee, Hoonah, Juneau, Haines, and Skagway.

Following are truly off-the-beaten-path camping opportunities along the routes of these vessels.

Hyder. For travelers planning trips north on the Alaska Marine Highway there is one very well known boarding point (Seattle), one fairly well identified (Prince Rupert, British Columbia), and there is one that hardly anybody has ever heard of—Hyder. Actually, for the adventuresome traveler who enjoys getting away from the madding throng, Hyder is probably the embarkation port of choice. The smaller ferry *Aurora* calls at Hyder once each week and delivers passengers and vehicles to Ketchikan via the incredibly beautiful Portland Canal fjord. Hyder, Alaska, and the abutting community of Stewart, British Columbia, Canada, are accessed by a short road leading from British Columbia's north-south Cassiar Highway. Stewart, at nine hundred hardy souls, is the larger of the two communities. Hyder boasts one hundred residents.

Camping is at **Raine Creek Park** on the Canada side of the border. It contains toilets, picnic facilities, hot showers, and dump station. At Hyder on the Alaska side of the border, the **Canal Trading Post** offers a limited number of RV spaces. The trading post proprietor, incidentally, is Dave Stevens, manager-owner of Alaska-Yukon RV Caravans. (See page 27.)

At press time the Hyder community association is constructing a community campground, but completion date of the project is not known.

Metlakatla, Kake, Angoon, Pelican, and Tenakee Springs. These communities are not really equipped to handle RVs, even if self-contained. Spokespersons advised the authors that camping visits are not encouraged.

At Pelican and Tenakee Springs, vehicles cannot even be off-loaded from the ferries. (At Tenakee Springs, however, there are tenting spaces at Indian River about a mile east of town; but be on the lookout for bears, especially when the salmon are running.)

In spite of the lack of RV facilities, these communities are not off-limits to visitors. To the contrary, all of these places contain adequate hotel-motel overnight accommodations for the traveler who wants a glimpse into southeastern Alaska's really rural lifestyles.

Hollis and Prince of Wales Island. This is real off-the-beaten-path country—but very much an option for the traveler. Prince of Wales Island is the third largest in the nation (after Kodiak Island, Alaska, and the big island of Hawaii).

It is also the site of major logging activity over the past three decades. As a result of logging, seven hundred miles of roads have been established, especially in the northern two-thirds of the island.

For the fisherman Prince of Wales offers frequent freshwater opportunities for Dolly Varden; cutthroat trout; rainbows; red, pink, chum, and silver salmon. All of these fish plus king salmon and steelhead trout are also available in saltwater bays and inlets.

The USFS publishes an excellent free road guide and map of Prince of Wales Island. It is available from district rangers at Craig and Thorne Bay on the island or from the USFS Supervisor, Tongass National Forest, Federal Building, Ketchikan, Alaska 99901.

Road conditions vary but generally the paved Big Salt and Thorne Bay roads running east-west across the middle of the island and the main gravel roads elsewhere are relatively easy to negotiate. Caution: Some small spurs may have no turnouts or convenient turnaround places; no problem for most RVs but they might be difficult for vehicles pulling long travel trailers.

Be on the lookout everywhere for logging trucks. They have the

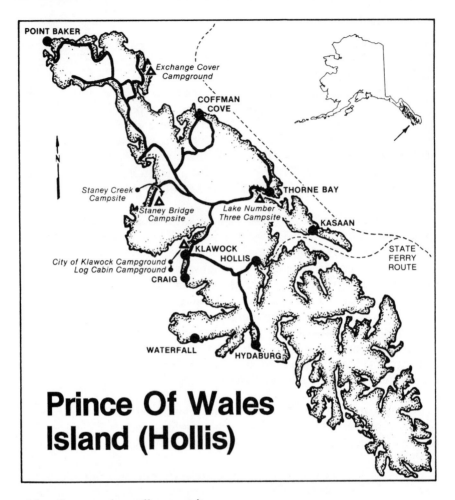

POINT BAKER

Exchange Cover
Campground

COFFMAN
COVE

N

Staney Creek
Campsite

Staney Bridge
Campsite

THORNE BAY

Lake Number
Three Campsite

KASAAN

KLAWOCK
HOLLIS

STATE
FERRY
ROUTE

City of Klawock Campground
Log Cabin Campground

CRAIG

WATERFALL

HYDABURG

Prince Of Wales
Island (Hollis)

right-of-way and usually assert it.

You stand a pretty good chance of seeing black bears, beavers, and Sitka black-tailed deer during a sojourn around this island. If you are real lucky you may catch a fleeting glance at a wolf. Geese, ducks, swans, and other waterfowl use Prince of Wales' many lakes and ponds for nesting and resting. Eagles may be seen at salt water's edge.

You can also see the effects of substantial logging for spruce, hemlock, and cedar. Many conservationists cite this island as overlogged and under-protected and they say it shows. Developers say reforestation is coming along nicely, thank you. You be the judge.

Ferry service to and from Hollis, a former logging camp on Prince of Wales Island, is almost daily in the summertime. Service is on the *Aurora*, out of Ketchikan, and the crossing around and between dozens of big and little islands takes close to three hours. There are five designated public camping areas on the island, plus one commercial campground. South to north, the first of these is the municipal **City of Klawock Campground** in Klawock on the west coast of the island. Klawock is the first community you come to driving westerly from Hollis on state highway 924. Eight spaces are available there within easy driving distance of grocery stores, gas station, fishing lodges, and boat charter operations. There is a daily $5 fee. **Log Cabin Campground**, a commercial facility with full hookups, is also located in Klawock.

Other campgrounds are operated by the USFS, which has jurisdiction over most of the island.

Northeast of Klawock on Lake Ellen Road is **Lake Number Three Campsite**. You get to Lake Ellen Road from Klawock by driving the paved state highway 929 (Big Salt Road), and the paved forest development road number 30 (Thorne Bay Road), to a southerly turnoff about 6.5 miles west of the town of Thorne Bay.

Like other USFS campgrounds on the island, this one is small (2 units), has toilets, picnic tables, and fireplaces, but no garbage disposal or water. There is no fee for using any of the USFS sites.

The other three USFS campgrounds are located off North Island Road, a north-meandering route, which the USFS designates as forest development road number 20. About 5 miles from North Island Road's junction with Big Salt and Thorne Bay roads, access roads bearing the numbers 2050, 2050-200, and 2050-500 lead to **Staney Bridge Campsite**. About 6 miles farther along North Island Road you come to another access road, number 2054. About a mile down this road you come to a fork. You can drive to the left and take forest road number 2050-500 to the Staney Bridge Campsite mentioned above, or you can head to the right on 2054 and arrive at **Horseshoe Hole Campsite**, also known as **Staney Creek Campsite** (not far from salt water).

About 40 miles north along the North Island Road you come to east-heading forest development road number 25, which leads to the small community of Whale Pass. There, road number 30 leads 16 miles to **Exchange Cove Campground** near the top of Prince of Wales Island.

Gasoline can be hard to come by on Prince of Wales Island. It is sold only at Klawock, Craig, Whale Pass, and Thorne Bay. Watch your fuel consumption carefully and top off your tank whenever the opportunity presents itself.

Hoonah. A village of mostly Indian peoples, Hoonah is located on the forested northeast shore of Chichagof Island. The community lies some forty miles west of Juneau and is a regular port of call (twice weekly northbound, twice weekly southbound) for the Alaska ferry *LaConte*. Like other southeastern Alaska Indian villages, the community relies heavily on fishing for its cash economy.

A cafe, bar, and lodge are established there, as are grocery and gasoline services. Although the city has no developed campground, RVers can park their rigs overnight at the harbor. There is no charge. Washing and limited shower facilities are nearby.

The Haines Highway to the Yukon Territory (Alaska Highway 7, British Columbia Highway 4, and Yukon Highway 3)

The Haines Highway, sometimes still called the Haines Cutoff, runs 150 miles from the city of Haines in southeastern Alaska's coastal region to Haines Junction, Yukon Territory, on the Alaska Highway. (Haines Junction is 90-plus miles west of Whitehorse.)

The 40 miles of the route that lie in Alaska are paved. About half of the remaining road in Canada is also paved. Most of the other half is gravel but in the process of being hard-surfaced. There are several slow-driving construction areas and a few short detours. The latter can be muddy if it is raining, and bumpy anytime, but not really difficult to negotiate.

It is a fascinating road to travel. In the course of one day's drive you ascend from a sea-level maritime locale of thick evergreens and islands to a much higher, drier, alpine environment of mountain plateaus and sparse vegetation.

The peaks you pass by are frequently sawtoothed and spectacular. Even in late July you will look *down* on snow patches in rifts and gullies. At the northern end of the road you are in Canada's Kluane National Park where marked hiking trails into the park's interior take off at frequent intervals along the roadway.

The road is part of the so-called Alaska-Yukon Golden Circle: a route that utilizes the full length of the Haines Highway, a 90-mile segment of the Alaska Highway from Haines Junction to Whitehorse, and then the 97-mile Klondike Highway from Whitehorse to Skagway. The circle is completed with a one-hour ferry trip back to Haines.

Your itinerary along the entire circuit provides a never-ending delight of mountains, pristine lakes, historic gold rush sites, unsurpassed fishing opportunities, and, not infrequently, the chance to meet and know some of the modern pioneers who choose to live in this part of the North Country.

The circle route provides a particularly pleasant option for round-trip ferry or cruise ship passengers who can rent RVs in Haines.

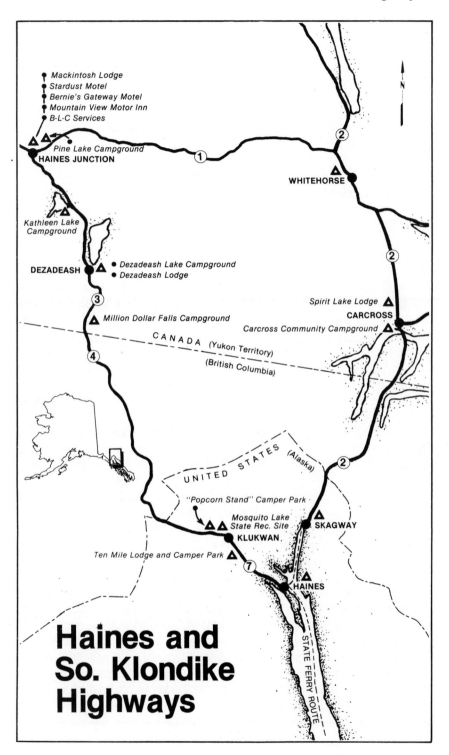

Mackintosh Lodge
Stardust Motel
Bernie's Gateway Motel
Mountain View Motor Inn
B-L-C Services

Pine Lake Campground
HAINES JUNCTION

1

2

WHITEHORSE

Kathleen Lake
Campground

2

DEZADEASH
Dezadeash Lake Campground
Dezadeash Lodge

3

Spirit Lake Lodge

CARCROSS

Million Dollar Falls Campground

Carcross Community Campground

CANADA (Yukon Territory)
(British Columbia)

4

2

"Popcorn Stand" Camper Park

UNITED STATES (Alaska)

Mosquito Lake
State Rec. Site
KLUKWAN

SKAGWAY

Ten Mile Lodge and Camper Park

7

HAINES

STATE FERRY ROUTE

Haines and
So. Klondike
Highways

Within or near the city of Haines are a rich variety of public and private camper parks, including Chilkat State Park and Chilkoot Lake State Recreation Area (see pages 48–49). Here are campgrounds along the Haines Highway.

TEN MILE LODGE AND CAMPER PARK (private)
Mile 10 Haines Highway

"POPCORN STAND" CAMPER PARK (private)
Mile 27 Haines Highway

MOSQUITO LAKE STATE RECREATION SITE (Alaska State Parks)
Access road at Mile 27 Haines Highway

Do not let the name scare you. This campground—the last public wayside on the Alaska side of the border if you are heading north to Canada, and the first if you are coming south—harbors no more mosquitoes than any other. Nine camping units are located here, along with toilets, spring water, picnic shelter and facilities, a boat ramp, and a boat dock.

If you carry a canoe or boat, visit the far end of the lake. It is much prettier than the end near the campground. Fishing in the lake produces Dollies, cutthroat, sockeye and silver salmon. You may see bears or mountain goats in the area.

Caution: This campground is off the highway and accessible by a 2.7-mile road. A pretty steep driveway with a rather sharp bend at the end could be troublesome for a big travel trailer. No fee; 7-day camping limit.

At Mile 40 you come to the United States-Canada border. Adjust your clocks and watches. Alaska operates on Alaska time; British Columbia and the Yukon Territory operate on Pacific time. When it is noon in Alaska, it is 1:00 P.M. on the Canada side of the boundary.

To pass into Canada you have to pass through Canada customs (or, if you are heading to Alaska, you have to stop at United States customs). Canada customs is open from 8:00 A.M. until midnight, Pacific time. United States Customs is open during exactly the same time period but on the United States side of the border it is 7:00 A.M. until 11:00 P.M., Alaska time.

From Mile 40 to Mile 87, you are in British Columbia and the Alaskan mileposts become Canadian metric kilometerposts. We will list distances here in kilometers as the signposts do, with mileage distances from Haines in brackets. At Kilometer 154 (Mile 87) you cross the line from the province of British Columbia to the Yukon Territory.

MILLION DOLLAR FALLS CAMPGROUND (Yukon government)
Kilometer 167.2 (Mile 102.7) Haines Highway

This first campground in the Yukon provides marvelous opportunities to view and photograph cascading falls and mountain vistas of the Saint Elias Range. There are trails, campsites for 27 parties, fire grates, drinking water, toilets, kids' playground with obstacle course, 2 kitchen shelters, and separate day-use picnic area and group fire pit.

To reach the campground you drive a ¼-mile, sometimes washboard-surface, access road. The campground is on a high plateau overlooking a deep gorge. Be very careful to stay on established trails. Taking off on your own on trails that appear to be game paths or open passes through the brush could be precarious—even fatal. It is a long, long way down. Camping fee is $5 per night.

DEZADEASH LODGE (private)
Kilometer 202 (Mile 125) Haines Highway

DEZADEASH LAKE CAMPGROUND (Yukon government)
Kilometer 205 (Mile 127) Haines Highway

Set on a small spit jutting into the waters of Dezadeash (pronounced DEZ-a-dee-ash) Lake—where northern pike, lake trout, and grayling come in the whopper category—the campground provides 10 camping spaces, tables, fire grates, boat launch, but no drinking water. This is mostly an open-area campground, with spaces not really defined. Trees and vegetation are sparse, which gives you a better view of the lake. On windy days, waves lap up on the gravel beach. (In 1986 the northbound highway sign and arrow indicating the road to this site was missing.) Camping fee is $5.

KATHLEEN LAKE CAMPGROUND (Parks Canada)
Kilometer 229 (Mile 142) Haines Highway

This is the only developed campground within Canada's big, spectacular, wild Kluane National Park. Forty-two camping spaces are located here, along with toilet facilities, kitchen area, fireplaces, tables, boat launch, and a range of interpretative programs by park rangers. Fishing is good in the lake for lake trout, grayling, and rainbows (in the Kathleen River).

Set in a thick forest of trembling aspen and spruce, at the base of a massive mountain of the Kluane Range, the campground has a great wilderness atmosphere. Camping fee is $5 per night, payable in envelopes available at the park entrance to an "iron ranger" receptacle.

PINE LAKE CAMPGROUND (Yukon government)
Kilometer 1629 (Mile 1013) Alaska Highway

This is Haines Junction's closest public campground. Note that it is approximately 6 kilometers east of Haines Junction on the Alaska, not the Haines, Highway. It is situated on Pine Lake, with a view of the Saint Elias mountains. The timber seems extraordinarily tall here, and in late July/August there are grand profusions of fireweed. No question about it, this is our choice for camping around Haines Junction.

The campground has 33 RV campsites (including pull-throughs) plus 10 sites for tents close to a great sandy beach. A sign indicates swimming here, but it looks *cold.* Test the temperature before you dive. Also on site: kitchen shelter, group fire pits, playground, tables, drinking water, and toilet facilities. Boat launching and docking facilities are a feature of the lake's man-made beach. We have noted more firewood cut and stacked here than at any other public campground in the Yukon or Alaska. Camping fee is $5.

Following are private campgrounds within or near Haines Junction, which is located at Kilometer 255.8 (Mile 159) when measured from Haines, Alaska. The junction is at Kilometer 1635 (Mile 1016) along the Alaska Highway.

B-L-C SERVICES (private)

MOUNTAIN VIEW MOTOR INN (private)

BERNIE'S GATEWAY MOTEL (private)
All located on the Alaska Highway within the community of Haines Junction.

STARDUST MOTEL (private)
Kilometer 1636.3 (Mile 1017) Alaska Highway

MACINTOSH LODGE (private)
Kilometer 1644.7 (Mile 1022) Alaska Highway

The Klondike Highway, Skagway to Whitehorse (Alaska Highway 2 and British Columbia/Yukon Highway 2)

The Klondike Highway is another "adventure road" through mountain passes, alongside sparkling streams, and into historic gold rush locales. This portion of the road is paved for its 98-mile length from Skagway at southeastern tidewater to Whitehorse, the capital city of the Yukon Territory.

Actually, it almost seems as if there are *two* Klondike Highways. What we are covering in this chapter is the southern segment, which terminates at a junction with the Alaska Highway a few miles south of Whitehorse. In Chapter 3 we will describe camping and trailering along the 324-mile northern portion, which commences at another junction on the Alaska Highway a few miles north of the Yukon's largest city. The northern portion leads to Dawson City in the Klondike River country.

The first dozen miles of road out of Skagway are pretty steep and curvy, but after they are behind you the going gets comfortable. From time to time the railroad tracks of the now-inoperative White Pass and Yukon Route narrow-gauge railway are visible across the canyon to your right as you ascend. The railroad, constructed during the late 1800s, was one of the great engineering and construction feats of the nineteenth century. It was carved out of the mountains, utilizing tons of black blasting powder and no small measure of human courage. In order to place the charges, the men were often lowered by rope over the sides of steep and precarious cliffs.

Like the Haines Highway, the Klondike route passes through Alaska, British Columbia, and the Yukon Territory. The United States customs station is at Mile 5.7 (open 7:00 A.M. to 11:00 P.M., Alaska time) and the United States-Canada border is at Mile 14.8. Canada customs officials are located at Kilometer 35.6 (Mile 22.1 from Skagway), and they operate from 8:00 A.M. until midnight, Pacific time.

There are only two campgrounds on the Klondike Highway south of Whitehorse.

CARCROSS COMMUNITY CAMPGROUND (city of Carcross)
Access road at Kilometer 106 (Mile 66) Klondike Highway

Located at the junction of the Klondike Highway and Tagish Road on the west end of Nares Lake, the community-maintained campground contains 12 campsites. There is no developed water supply.

SPIRIT LAKE LODGE (private)
Kilometer 116 (Mile 72) Klondike Highway

For a listing of campgrounds in and around Whitehorse, see pages 69–70. For campgrounds along the Klondike Highway north of Whitehorse en route to Dawson City, see pages 73–79.

3

The Alaska Highway
and the Yukon Territory

A trip to Alaska and the Yukon is in a category with some of the earth's great vacation journeys.

A key ingredient (some would say *the* key ingredient) that makes this so is the Alaska Highway.

And what makes the Alaska Highway special is the country it goes through. When at last you have traveled all the approach roads and you enter this part of the North Country, you will find yourself in a still wondrously wild terrain. Get off the road a few miles (or even a few hundred feet in many places) and you are in a primitive and seemingly endless land of untouched timber, tundra, marshes, and mountains. To the extent that it is peopled, it is a country of homesteaders, prospectors, and other pioneer folk trying to wring a living out of a tough, harsh frontier. Get off the road in other places and there are no people at all—just grizzly bears, wolves, moose, caribou, and other wild creatures.

All of which makes this ideal country for the RV traveler. From the vantage point of your mobile shelter you can witness and enjoy the wilderness immensely. Indeed, you are yourself immersed in it. Yet within the comfort of your unit you are ever safe, warm, and dry.

The Alaska Highway (Alaskans never call it the Alcan) begins at Dawson Creek, British Columbia—not to be confused with Dawson City in the Yukon Territory. It ends, at least as far as most travelers, guidebooks, and northerners are concerned, roughly fifteen hundred miles later at Fairbanks, Alaska. (It really ends at Mile 1422 in Delta Junction, but we will discuss that in Chapter 4.)

The road is now some four decades old, having been constructed during World War II as a military supply route. Incredibly, traffic began using the route only eight months after the road building began.

The highway was first opened for public use in 1948. It was, until recent years, an almost entirely gravel highway. Now the road is totally paved in Alaska and it is mostly paved in Canada. Further, it is being improved all the time. Be alert nonetheless for potholes in both gravel and pavement. Be alert, too, for long and short stretches of washboard surfaces in the gravel and for frost heaves in the pavement. These latter are rises and falls created by winter freezes and thaws. The effect can be rather like a roller coaster, so keep your speed moderate at all times.

Especially on gravel, keep your headlights on even during daylight hours. And keep to the right on curves and hills. The Alaska Highway is strictly a two-lane road, and often a narrow two lanes at that.

The easy way to keep track of where you are and where you want to go is by looking at the mileposts-kilometerposts beside the road. They are located every few miles, or kilometers, on the right side of the road heading northerly. In Canada the numbers represent kilometers from the highway's starting point in Dawson Creek, British Columbia. In Alaska the numbers represent miles, also starting from Dawson Creek.

The numbers, by the way, are no longer 100 percent accurate. Straightening out curves in the road from place to place has reduced the length of the highway by thirty miles or so. However, you can still ascertain with a fair degree of accuracy where you are and how far away your destination lies.

Mile and kilometer distances listed here are based on the posted numbers, not the actual distance from Dawson Creek.

Since this is a guide to campgrounds in Alaska and Canada's Yukon Territory, our listing begins at Kilometer 941.6 (Mile 588.2), the British Columbia-Yukon Territory border. The highway meanders east-west for several miles at this point, running parallel to and crisscrossing six times the east-west border. Thus we have campgrounds located in the Yukon, then British Columbia, then the Yukon again.

In the first part of this chapter, we list the Yukon highways that get the most visitor traffic each summer: the Alaska Highway from the British Columbia-Yukon Territory border to Alaska and the Klondike Highway segment from Whitehorse to Dawson City. In the last part of this chapter, beginning with the Top of the World Highway, we discuss campgrounds that are located on less-utilized roads in the territory.

These are truly off-the-beaten-path routes. Asphalt is but a memory along these roadways and on some of them gravel surfaces can be rougher, less maintained, and less comfortable than the gravel portions of the Yukon's principal highways.

For the adventurous soul, these are marvelous paths to see and explore, well worth the caution of carrying extra fuel and extra food in anticipation of greater distances between services and supplies. The mountains, lakes, and rivers seem all the more striking, all the more memorable because of their relative isolation. This is grand country. Well worth a shade less comfort, a little more effort and preparation to visit.

The fee for camping in Yukon government campgrounds is five dollars daily for nonresidents; season permits are twenty-five dollars. Campground permits are available from visitor reception centers at Watson Lake, Whitehorse, Carcross, Beaver Creek, Haines Junction, and Dawson City. They can also be obtained from the cash desk at the Yukon Government Building in Whitehorse, and Fish and Wildlife district offices in Whitehorse, Watson Lake, Ross River, Mayo, Dawson City, and Haines Junction. You can also buy them on-site from campground personnel.

A word about Yukon government campgrounds: We have found them to be almost uniformly excellent. Almost without exception they are situated beside some pleasant water body—a creek, a lake, perhaps even the Yukon River—and all of them contain picnic tables, fire grates, and toilet facilities (usually clean and well-tended outhouses, not flushing units). Almost all have water wells on-site. If you are camped where there is no well, be sure to boil the stream or lake water before drinking it. There are, incidentally, no camping limits at Yukon government campgrounds.

The fishing at many of the lakes can be first rate, but the real lunkers are generally available only from a boat. Caution: Savage windstorms can arise suddenly and without warning on many of the large Yukon (and for that matter, Alaskan) lakes. Do not take small boats too far from shore. And by all means wear a flotation device whenever you are on the water.

Following are public and private campgrounds from your first crossing into the Yukon Territory until you arrive in Alaska.

The Alaska Highway (British Columbia Highway 97, Yukon Highway 1)

CONTACT CREEK LODGE (private)
Kilometer 950 (Mile 590) Alaska Highway

IRON CREEK LODGE (private)
Kilometer 960 (Mile 596) Alaska Highway

HYLAND RIVER PROVINCIAL PARK (British Columbia
**   government)**
Kilometer 974.8 (Mile 602) Alaska Highway

The river on which this park is located provides reportedly fair to good angling for Dolly Varden, char, and grayling. The campground itself is a large parking/camping gravel pad with toilets, fireplaces, picnic facilities, and river access. Since the British Columbia parks people classify this as a wilderness camp there is no charge. There is a 14-day camping limit.

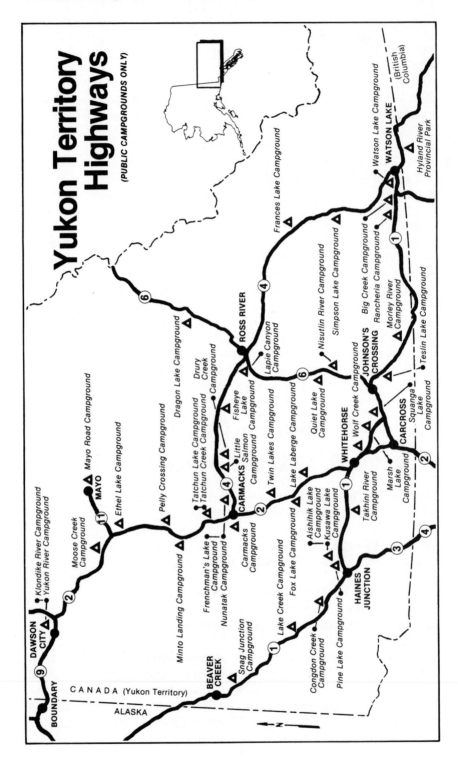

Yukon Territory Highways (PUBLIC CAMPGROUNDS ONLY)

CAMP-GROUND SERVICES (private)
Kilometer 1015 (Mile 632.5) Alaska Highway

At Kilometer 1020 (Mile 634) the Alaska Highway junctions with the Campbell Highway which leads northwesterly to a point near Carmacks on the Klondike Highway. For a listing of campgrounds along this route, see pages 80–82.

WATSON LAKE CAMPGROUND (Yukon government)
Kilometer 1025 (Mile 637) Alaska Highway

Watson Lake is the site of the famous, and rather incredible, forest of signs touting towns from virtually every state and province and from many foreign countries. The turnoff to the lakeside campground is a couple of miles beyond the signs. It contains 35 RV camping units plus 6 tent sites. The area also contains a kitchen shelter, toilets, drinking water, fireplaces, and boat launch. Hiking trails are also accessible from the campground. Daily camping fee is $5.

GREEN VALLEY TRAILER PARK (private)
Kilometer 1031.7 (Mile 640) Alaska Highway

JUNCTION 37 SERVICES (private)
Kilometer 1044 (Mile 649) Alaska Highway

IKE'S ISLAND (private)
Kilometer 1044.2 (Mile 649) Alaska Highway

BIG CREEK CAMPGROUND (Yukon government)
Kilometer 1084.6 (Mile 674) Alaska Highway

Located next to Big Creek, the campground contains 25 wooded campsites, drinking water, toilets, and a kitchen shelter. Daily camping fee is $5.

RANCHERIA HOTEL/MOTEL (private)
Kilometer 1143.4 (Mile 710) Alaska Highway

RANCHERIA CAMPGROUND (Yukon government)
Kilometer 1143.4 (Mile 710) Alaska Highway

Situated alongside the rather oddly named Rancheria River, the campground contains 12 campsites, drinking water, toilets, fireplaces, and a kitchen shelter. Daily camping fee is $5.

THE MESSAGE POST (private)
Kilometer 1154.7 (Mile 717) Alaska Highway

Tent camping only.

THE GREAT DIVIDE LODGE (private)
Kilometer 1160 (Mile 721) Alaska Highway

RAINBOW'S INN (private)
Kilometer 1161 (Mile 721) Alaska Highway

MORLEY RIVER CAMPGROUND (Yukon government)
Kilometer 1251.2 (Mile 777) Alaska Highway

Another riverside campground, this one contains 12 campsites, toilets, drinking water and, according to government publications, "good fishing" for northern pike, grayling, and lake trout. Daily camping fee is $5.

MORLEY RIVER LODGE (private)
Kilometer 1251.2 (Mile 777) Alaska Highway

THE TERI-TORI CAMPGROUND (private)
Kilometer 1281 (Mile 797) Alaska Highway

HALSTEAD'S (private)
Kilometer 1296.8 (Mile 807) Alaska Highway

TESLIN LAKE CAMPGROUND (Yukon government)
Kilometer 1307.7 (Mile 813.1) Alaska Highway

This site overlooks Teslin Lake and contains 19 camping units in a timbered setting. Available are drinking water, toilets, fireplaces, and a kitchen shelter. There is a boat launch about 1/3 mile north of the campground. Fishing in the area is for lake trout, grayling, northern pike, and whitefish. Daily camping fee is $5.

At Kilometer 1344.9 (Mile 836), the Alaska Highway junctions with the Canol Road. For a listing of campgrounds along this route, see pages 82–83.

JOHNSON'S CROSSING CAMPGROUND SERVICES (private)
Kilometer 1347 (Mile 837) Alaska Highway

SQUANGA LAKE CAMPGROUND (Yukon government)
Kilometer 1368.4 (Mile 850.5) Alaska Highway

A dozen campsites are located along the shores of Squanga Lake, plus a kitchen shelter, drinking water, toilets, and a boat launch for small craft. Angling is for burbot, northern pike, grayling, and whitefish. Daily camping fee is $5.

At Kilometer 1392.5 (Mile 866) you come to a junction called Jake's Corner. The junction leads to the Atlin and Tagish roads. For campgrounds along these highways, see pages 87–88.

LAKEVIEW RESORT AND MARINA (private)
Kilometer 1414 (Mile 879.5) Alaska Highway

MARSH LAKE CAMPGROUND (Yukon government)
Kilometer 1432 (Mile 890) Alaska Highway

Located approximately 30 miles south of Whitehorse, this is one of the Yukon's most pleasant camping places. An excellent day-use sandy beach is located here along with clothes-changing rooms, playground, picnic area, kitchen shelter, boat launch, plus drinking water and toilets. The day-use area is connected by trail to the camping section where 47 camping units, some of them pull-throughs, are located. Also in the area is another kitchen shelter, drinking water, toilets, tent spaces, and group fire pit. Daily camping fee is $5.

SOURDOUGH R.V. PARK AND CAMPSITE (private)
Kilometer 1454.5 (Mile 904) Alaska Highway

At Kilometer 1456 (Mile 905) the Alaska Highway junctions with the Klondike Highway which leads south to Skagway, Alaska. For a listing of campgrounds along this route, see pages 60–61.

WOLF CREEK CAMPGROUND (Yukon government)
Kilometer 1458 (Mile 907) Alaska Highway

Wolf Creek Campground is located 18 kilometers (11 miles) from Whitehorse and contains 38 campsites (some of them pull-throughs), a tenting area, 2 kitchen shelters, water, toilets, and a playground. Daily camping fee is $5.

PIONEER TRAILER PARK (private)
Kilometer 1465.7 (Mile 911) Alaska Highway

ROBERT SERVICE TENT CAMPGROUND (private)
About 2.6 kilometers (1.5 miles) east on South Access Road, which junctions with Alaska Highway at Kilometer 1470 (Mile 913).

SOURDOUGH CITY R.V. PARK (private)
Located on 2nd Avenue, north of Ogilvie, Whitehorse.

At Kilometer 1487.8 (Mile 924.5) the Alaska Highway junctions with the Klondike Highway north to Dawson City. For a listing of campgrounds along this route, see pages 73–79.

TAKHINI HOT SPRINGS (private)
Kilometer 10 (Mile 6) on Takhini Hot Springs Road, which junctions with the Klondike Highway at Kilometer 198 (Mile 123).

Located 17 miles from downtown Whitehorse, this campground offers excellent facilities; individual, separated spaces with tables and fire grates in a wooded setting. Some of the spaces are pull-throughs and some have electric hookups. Best of all, it also offers swimming and relaxing in a tension-relieving, odorless, 100° hot springs pool. Camping fee is $5, $7 with electric hookup.

TAKHINI RIVER CAMPGROUND (Yukon government)
Located 14.5 kilometers (9 miles) south on Kusawa Lake Road, which junctions with Alaska Highway at Kilometer 1542.7 (Mile 958.6).

This is a relatively small but pleasant campground in the woods. There are 7 units on the banks of the Takhini River. The road to this campground (and the Kusawa Lake Campground beyond it) has recently been widened and upgraded by the Yukon government. On-site are water and toilets. Daily camping fee is $5.

KUSAWA LAKE CAMPGROUND (Yukon government)
Located 22.5 kilometers (14 miles) south of Alaska Highway on Kusawa Lake Road.

Five miles down the Kusawa Lake Road beyond the Takhini River Campground is this site; a favorite with Yukoners and Alaskans in spite of (or perhaps because of) its relative isolation. Situated on the north end of the lake, the grounds include a day-use area on a sandy beach with boat dock, picnic sites, kitchen shelter, drinking water, and toilets. You are in forest surroundings here, and across the lake rise dramatic mountains. Use a spotting scope, and the chances are good you will see mountain sheep on the slopes. The campground has 22 campsites, a kitchen shelter, drinking water, toilets, and group fire pits. Daily camping fee is $5.

AISHIHIK LAKE CAMPGROUND (Yukon government)
Located on a side road 43 kilometers (27 miles) from junction with Alaska Highway at Kilometer 1602.3 (Mile 995.6).

Situated on the south end of Aishihik Lake, this campground offers 13 campsites, a group camping area, kitchen shelter, boat launch, playground, and good fishing for trophy lake trout.

To get to the big fish, however, you do need a boat. Be cautious, however; deadly windstorms can come up on the water without warning. Do not take a small boat too far from shore. Daily camping fee is $5.

PINE LAKE CAMPGROUND (Yukon government)
Kilometer 1629 (Mile 1013) Alaska Highway

Located approximately 6 kilometers east of Haines Junction, the campground is situated on Pine Lake with a view of the Saint Elias mountains. It is Haines Junction's nearest public campground. The timber seems extraordinarily tall here, and in late July/August there are grand profusions of fireweed.

The campground has 33 RV campsites, including pull-throughs, plus 10 additional tent sites close to a great sandy beach. A sign nearby indicates swimming—for the hardy. Also on-site: kitchen shelter, group fire pits, tables, playground, drinking water, lots of cut firewood, and toilets. Boat launching and docking facilities are also a feature of the lake's man-made beach. Daily camping fee is $5.

At Kilometer 1635.1, the Alaska Highway junctions with the Haines Highway leading south to Haines, Alaska. For a listing of campgrounds along this route, see pages 56–60.

The following five listings are private campgrounds within or near Haines Junction, which is located at Kilometer 1635 (Mile 1016) along the Alaska Highway.

B-L-C SERVICES (private)
Located within the community of Haines Junction.

MOUNTAIN VIEW MOTOR INN (private)
Located within the community of Haines Junction.

BERNIE'S GATEWAY MOTEL (private)
Located within the community of Haines Junction.

STARDUST MOTEL (private)
Kilometer 1636.3 (Mile 1017) Alaska Highway

MACINTOSH LODGE (private)
Kilometer 1644 (Mile 1022) Alaska Highway

KLUANE LAKE LODGE (private)
Kilometer 1699 (Mile 1056) Alaska Highway

BAYSHORE MOTEL AND RESTAURANT (private)
Kilometer 1711.7 (Mile 1064) Alaska Highway

COTTONWOOD PARK (private)
Kilometer 1717 (Mile 1067) Alaska Highway

CONGDON CREEK CAMPGROUND (Yukon government)
Kilometer 1724.8 (Mile 1071.7) Alaska Highway

This is another of our favorite camping spots. The campground is located on the wooded shores of Kluane (pronounced Clue-ON-ee) Lake— the Yukon's biggest. Seventy-seven RV and tent sites are located here along with 2 kitchen shelters, group fire pit, playground, boat launch, drinking water, and toilets. Some evenings, Kluane National Park rangers give interpretative talks about the mountains, woods, and wildlife of the area. On other occasions they conduct guided hikes up the Congdon Creek trail. Daily camping fee is $5.

BURWASH LANDING RESORT (private)
Kilometer 1759 (Mile 1093) Alaska Highway

KLUANE WILDERNESS VILLAGE (private)
Kilometer 1798 (Mile 1118) Alaska Highway

PINE VALLEY MOTEL (private)
Kilometer 1845.9 (Mile 1147) Alaska Highway

LAKE CREEK CAMPGROUND (Yukon government)
Kilometer 1853.7 (Mile 1152.1) Alaska Highway

Located next to Lake Creek, the campground contains 16 campsites, kitchen shelter, drinking water, toilets, and fireplaces. Daily camping fee is $5.

KOIDERN RIVER FISHING LODGE (private)
Kilometer 1873 (Mile 1164) Alaska Highway

KOIDERN GULF SERVICES (private)
Kilometer 1876 (Mile 1167) Alaska Highway

WHITE RIVER LODGE (private)
Kilometer 1881.3 (Mile 1169) Alaska Highway

SNAG JUNCTION CAMPGROUND (Yukon government)
Kilometer 1912 (Mile 1188.8) Alaska Highway

This is the last public campground in Canada if you are heading north. Fifteen camping units are located near the shores of Small Lake. A small-boat launch is here as well as kitchen shelter, toilets, picnic tables, and fireplaces. Some folks like to take a quick swim in the lake.

FAR WEST GULF (private)
Kilometer 1934 (Mile 1202) Alaska Highway

CUSTOM CAMPGROUND (private)
Kilometer 1935 (Mile 1202) Alaska Highway

Note: Beaver Creek Customs and Immigration offices are located approximately thirty kilometers (twenty miles) south of the United States-Canada border. If you are southbound from Alaska entering Canada you must stop here and clear customs.

The Klondike Highway, Whitehorse to Dawson City (Yukon Highway 2)

We mentioned in Chapter 2 that, for trip planning purposes, it seems as though there are two Klondike Highways: one from Skagway in southeastern Alaska to a point on the Alaska Highway just south of Whitehorse, and another from a junction just north of Whitehorse to the Klondike gold rush town of Dawson City.

The Klondike Highway is paved for about 100 miles north of Whitehorse, then for the next 220 miles to Dawson City you run into alternating stretches of gravel, asphalt, or a hard-surface compound called chip-seal. Grades for the most part are moderate. You will parallel and be able to see the wide and awesome Yukon River at various points along the way. At Dawson City you will complete your journey by taking a ferry across the mighty stream.

SPECIAL NOTE ABOUT DRIVING TO ALASKA VIA THE TOP OF THE WORLD HIGHWAY

The Klondike Highway connects at Dawson City with the Top of the World Highway leading west to Alaska and the Taylor Highway. The Taylor, in turn, puts you back on the Alaska Highway at Tetlin Junction, just inside Alaska on the Alaska Highway. Thus, either coming to Alaska or going home, this Klondike Highway-Top of the World Highway-Taylor Highway loop provides an alternative to duplicating a lot of Alaska Highway miles.

If you are interested in this option our suggestion is that when you get to Whitehorse, heading north, check to see what the weather has been and is expected to be on the Top of the World portion of the trip. Heavy rains can make the otherwise-excellent clay surface on portions of the road quite slippery. If it has been relatively dry and heavy rains are not expected, you can drive the loop to Dawson and into Alaska that way.

On the other hand, if there has been lots of rain in recent days, we suggest you stick to the paved Alaska Highway, driving that road on into Alaska. When you are homeward bound and ready to leave Alaska, you can check again to see what the weather has been. If weather conditions have been fair or simply occasional light rains, then drive the Taylor Highway north from Tetlin Junction and take the Top of the World route. If there has been much rain, or if rain is expected, then you might want to bag the loop idea, drive to Whitehorse on the Alaska Highway, and simply drive the very negotiable Klondike Highway to Dawson City and back.

For road conditions and camping opportunities on the Top of the World Highway, see pages 79–80. For similar information about the Taylor Highway, see pages 131–134.

Following are campgrounds along the Klondike Highway from its junction with the Alaska Highway at Kilometer 1487.8 (Mile 924.5) on the Alaska Highway. Bear in mind that the Klondike Highway officially starts roughly 190 kilometers (118 miles) south of this junction at Skagway on the southeastern Alaska coast, so kilometerposts and mileposts along the way measure distance from there.

Before you head north on the Klondike Highway, be sure to check your gas level. The first refueling stop on the highway is nearly 60 miles down the road, and if for any reason it happens to be closed the station at Carmacks is another 47 miles.

TAKHINI HOT SPRINGS (private)
Kilometer 10 (Mile 6) on Takhini Hot Springs Road, which junctions
with the Klondike Highway at Kilometer 198 (Mile 123).

This is one of the Yukon's most pleasurable resting or camping areas. On the grounds are picnic areas, cafe, laundromats, 70 campsites (some with electric hookups), and terrific swimming in an odorless, wonderfully refreshing hot springs pool. Individual RV and tent spaces, with tables and fire grates, are set among spruce and birch trees. Some of the spaces are pull-throughs. Daily camping fee is $5.00; $7.50 with electric hookup.

LAKE LABERGE CAMPGROUND (Yukon government)
Kilometer 228 (Mile 141.7) Klondike Highway

Located on the lake made famous in a Robert Service poem (*The Cremation of Sam McGee*) and adjacent to a stream called Deep Creek, this campground contains 22 camping units plus kitchen shelter, boat launch, drinking water, and toilets. Angling is fair to good for lake trout and northern pike. Within earshot of the campground is an apparently large kennel of sled dogs. Be aware that at night they sometimes howl long and mightily. For some visitors this is a distressing annoyance; for others it is a delightful North Country experience. Daily camping fee is $5.

FOX LAKE CAMPGROUND (Yukon government)
Kilometer 248 (Mile 154.1) Klondike Highway

Government publications list this site as good fishing for lake trout, burbot, and grayling. The campground has 19 campsites, fire grates, tables, kitchen shelter, drinking water, and toilets. This is a large, scenic lake, and the campground is situated among tall conifers. A large gravel beach gives canoe or kayak access to the water. Daily camping fee is $5.

TWIN LAKES CAMPGROUND (Yukon government)
Kilometer 304.6 (Mile 189.3) Klondike Highway

A smaller campground, this facility has 8 camping units plus drinking water, toilets, fire grates, and boat launch. Yukon government guidebooks show this as a swimming lake but test the water with your toe first; it can be pretty chilly. This is an open gravel campground and vehicles park right next to the lake. Because trees and plants are sparse here, camping spaces are not separated. For this same reason it gets lots of sun. The haunting, trilling call of loons can sometimes be heard here. Daily camping fee is $5.

CARMACKS CAMPGROUND (Yukon government)
Kilometer 357.9 (Mile 222.4) Klondike Highway

Here is another chance to camp on the shores of the Yukon River, although we found these grounds a little less well maintained than at most Yukon government campgrounds.

This was the only place, for instance, where we found toilets without paper, and firewood was in short supply. Perhaps because it is situated only .25 mile from Carmacks shopping and services, the campground seemed a bit busy with traffic. Twice while we were there, local teenagers zoomed through in cars and motorbikes.

Twelve campsites are located here, along with kitchen shelter, tables, fire grates, toilets, and boat launch. There is a well on-site, but signs say to boil the water for 15 minutes before drinking it. This is a handy point for putting in or hauling out a canoe or kayak. Daily camping fee is $5.

Note: Check your fuel level; gas can be purchased in Carmacks but stations are infrequent both north and south of this community.

At Kilometer 360 (Mile 223.7), the Klondike Highway junctions with the Campbell Highway leading southeasterly to Watson Lake on the Alaska Highway. For a listing of campgrounds along this route, see pages 80–82.

TATCHUN CREEK CAMPGROUND (Yukon government)
Kilometer 383.5 (Mile 238.3) Klondike Highway

Located along the banks of Tatchun Creek, this 13-site campground offers fire pits, drinking water, toilets, and good grayling fishing. Daily camping fee is $5.

TATCHUN LAKE CAMPGROUND (Yukon government)
Located 8.5 kilometers (5 miles) on a side road that junctions with the Klondike Highway at Kilometer 385 (Mile 239).

Twenty campsites are maintained here along with kitchen shelter, picnic area, drinking water, toilets, and a boat launch. Fish in the lake include northern pike. Daily camping fee is $5.

MIDWAY LODGE (private)
Kilometer 424 (Mile 263.5) Klondike Highway

MINTO LANDING CAMPGROUND (Yukon government)
Located on a west-heading side road 2 kilometers (1.2 miles) from
junction with the Klondike Highway at Kilometer 431.5 (Mile 268.2).

If you are heading south there is no sign or arrow indicating the access
road to this campground and the community of Minto. It is, however,
another of the Yukon government's excellent water-related camping sites.
The water, in this instance, is the wide Yukon River.

The campground is located on a grassy riverbank and 10 campsites
have been established. The sites are not separated, and the area could easily
accommodate four times that number. Also available: kitchen shelter,
drinking water, fire grates, toilets, and a handy location for river travelers to
haul in or haul out their paddlecraft. An old gold rush log cabin still stands at
the area, ideal for picture taking. Daily camping fee is $5.

PELLY CROSSING CAMPGROUND (Selkirk Indian band)
Kilometer 465.2 (Mile 289.1) Klondike Highway

This is a largely unmaintained site on the wooded banks of the Pelly
River. Although spartan, it is certainly adequate for self-contained RVs. No
charge.

ETHEL LAKE CAMPGROUND (Yukon government)
Kilometer 27 (Mile 16) on an eastbound side road from junction at
Kilometer 526.8 (Mile 327) Klondike Highway

The access road to this 14-site campground is narrow and curvy; not
recommended for travel trailers or big rigs. There is a boat launch there and
government publications rate the area as good fishing. Daily camping fee
is $5.

STEWART CROSSING LODGE (private)
Kilometer 537.3 (Mile 333.9) Klondike Highway

At Kilometer 538.2 the Klondike Highway junctions with Yukon
Highway 11, the Silver Trail (formerly the Mayo Road). The following two
campgrounds are located along this road.

MAYO ROAD CAMPGROUND (Yukon government)
Located at Kilometer 53 (Mile 33) on the Silver Trail.

Located on the south banks of the Mayo River, within walking
distance of the small mining community of Mayo, this campground has 8

campsites, a kitchen shelter, and toilets. Water from the stream is drinkable, but should be boiled. Daily camping fee is $5.

An additional modest campground has been located at the Mayo Lake dam approximately 42 kilometers (26 miles) from Mayo. The Mayo Road is narrow and curvy in places but is not a difficult road to negotiate.

MOOSE CREEK CAMPGROUND (Yukon government)
Kilometer 562.5 (Mile 349.2) Klondike Highway

Here is a pleasant stopping place for lunch or overnight, set in thick stands of birch trees. Thirty-six separated campsites, some of them pull-throughs, plus tenting areas are located adjacent to Moose Creek and the Stewart River. A trail from the camping area leads to good fishing. In addition, the grounds contain a playground (with obstacle course, on which kids can work off excess energy), kitchen shelter, water, and toilets.

At Kilometer 678 (Mile 421.3), the Klondike Highway junctions with the Dempster Highway to Inuvik in the Northwest Territories. For a listing of campgrounds along this route, see pages 83–86.

KLONDIKE RIVER CAMPGROUND (Yukon government)
Kilometer 698 (Mile 433.8) Klondike Highway

This is an exceptional campground, and it can fill up early. Many campers check in, select and mark their sites with signs, ropes, or even stools and lawn chairs, then they head on to Dawson City just a dozen miles farther up the road. Generously sized campsites, some of them pull-throughs, are located among stands of very tall conifers.

Twenty-seven RVs can be accommodated here, and a wide gravel parking area near the entrance could handle a dozen more. The campground is located adjacent to Rock Creek and the Klondike River. A kitchen shelter, drinking water, tables, fire grates, and toilets are available here.

GUGGIEVILLE CAMPGROUND (private)
Located on Bonanza Creek Road from junction with Klondike Highway at Kilometer 714.2 (Mile 443.9).

GOLD RUSH CAMPGROUND (private)
Located at 5th and York Street, Dawson City.

YUKON RIVER CAMPGROUND (Yukon government)
Located on west side of the Yukon River, accessible from Dawson City by free ferry.

This is the Yukon's biggest government campground, providing 76 RV camping sites, 20 tent sites, 2 kitchen shelters, playground, drinking water, toilets—and the thrill of knowing you are at the site of one of the world's greatest, grandest gold stampedes. These sites are on the Yukon River, and individual spaces are separated from each other by stands of tall spruce and birch trees. Among the birches you occasionally come across individual trees whose trunk tops bend completely around in a sort of inverted "J" or fishhook shape.

Like the Klondike River Campground, this one can fill up early. Be aware that the ferry, which runs between the camping area and Dawson City, operates only between 9:00 A.M. and 9:00 P.M. If you were camped at the river campground but came across the river to take in Dawson City's 8:00 P.M. to 10:00 P.M. gold rush variety show, you would be stuck on the wrong side of the Yukon when you wanted to return to your campsite.

Top of the World Highway
(Yukon Highway 9)

This road has gone by several names over the years. To Yukoners it used to be the Sixty Mile Highway or the Dawson-Boundary Road. Many Alaskans thought of it as part of the Taylor Highway. For visitors driving this route, literally at high ridgetop level from one mountain to another, the nickname Top of the World Highway seemed most apt. In recent times the Yukon government has made Top of the World Highway the official territorial designation. Small wonder. Your view as you travel this road is frequently *down*, to forested valleys and rivers far, far below your mountainside perch. Near the end of the road, you are in an alpine environment where only the hardiest small trees and bushes can exist.

The highway is much wider, smoother, and easier to drive than its Alaskan counterpart, the Taylor Highway. Be advised, however, that in rainy weather this road can be slick. Under any conditions it is a road you should not try to drive in a hurry. Speeds of twenty to twenty-five miles per hour will be common along curves and narrow stretches; if the road is wet you will need to travel even slower. To reach the road from Dawson City, cross the Yukon River by the free ferry.

There is only one campground along the road, the Yukon River Campground (see pages 78–79).

At Kilometer 107.8 (Mile 67), you clear United States customs if you are heading west (or Canada customs if you are eastbound) and you are back in the United States again. Both customs offices are open twelve hours each day; 9:00 A.M. to 9:00 P.M. Pacific time in Canada, and 8:00 A.M. to 8:00 P.M. Alaska time in Alaska. Nearby is the community of Boundary where gas is available. Check your tank. Gas is not readily available on the Taylor Highway.

CORBETT'S BOUNDARY ROADHOUSE (private)
Kilometer 114.3 (Mile 71) Top of the World Highway

At Kilometer 130.3 (Mile 81) the highway junctions with the Taylor Highway. (See pages 131–134). You can head north at this point for a visit to historic Eagle or south to rejoin the Alaska Highway.

The Campbell Highway (Yukon Highway 4)

The nearly 350-mile Campbell Highway had its origins in the mid-1800s explorations of Robert Campbell. He traveled by foot and by boat in the Yukon, setting up trading posts as far away as Alaska.

The road that carries his name today follows his route in southeastern Yukon. It joins Watson Lake just inside the Yukon border on the Alaska Highway with Carmacks on the Klondike Highway. For campgrounds in or near Watson Lake, see pages 67–68. Following are campgrounds along the Campbell Highway.

SIMPSON LAKE CAMPGROUND (Yukon government)
Kilometer 83.1 (Mile 50) Campbell Highway

Situated scenically alongside Simpson Lake, the campground has 18 camping units, drinking water, fire grates, kitchen shelter, and toilets. If the kids want to run off some pent-up energy there is a playground and swimming beach. Boat launch and docking facilities are also on-site. Lake trout angling is reportedly superior. Camping fee is $5.

BEN AND WILMA'S PLACE (private)
Kilometer 108 (Mile 67) Campbell Highway

FRANCES LAKE CAMPGROUND (Yukon government)
Kilometer 176.5 (Mile 106.7) Campbell Highway

This campground is located 1 kilometer (.6 mile) west of the Campbell Highway. It is set on another lake rated as good fishing by the Yukon government. The camping area contains 17 campsites, drinking water, toilets, fire grates and tables, picnic kitchen shelter, and a boat launch. A single, very photogenic, peak rises more than 5,000 feet where the two arms of Frances Lake come together. Camping fee is $5.

At Kilometer 355.7 (Mile 221) the Campbell Highway junctions with the Canol Road. For campgrounds along this route, see pages 82–83.

LAPIE CANYON CAMPGROUND (Yukon government)
Kilometer 375 (Mile 226) Campbell Highway

Another of the North Country's real treasures, this campground is set in a splendid scenic canyon in a mixed forest of white and black spruce, lodgepole pine, balsam poplar, and trembling aspen. Along the rocky slopes of the 75-meter (245-foot) canyon walls you can spot the steel-blue color of juniper.

Fourteen well-spaced campsites are situated in these woods along the frothy Lapie River. Among on-site improvements are drinking water, toilets, fire grates, kitchen shelters, group fire pit, and a picnic area. Tenters have a special break; 4 walk-in tenting sites have been reserved on the lower level nearest the river. The river winds through forested areas and through steep-walled canyons with whirlpools and rapids. It is rated from grades II to IV for canoeists and kayakers, depending on water levels. Camping fee is $5.

FISHEYE LAKE CAMPGROUND (Yukon government)
Kilometer 403 (Mile 260) Campbell Highway

This is a small campground located 3 miles west of the Faro Road-Campbell Highway junction. The grounds contain 5 camping sites, toilets, and fire grates. You can swim in the lake. Rainbow trout were introduced into these waters by Yukon fish and game people. Camping fee is $5.

DRURY CREEK CAMPGROUND (Yukon government)
Kilometer 469.9 (Mile 292) Campbell Highway

Located on Drury Creek at the east end of Little Salmon Lake, this wooded wayside contains 18 camping units, drinking water, fire grates, toilets, kitchen shelter, group fire pit, boat launch, and even a fish filleting table—further evidence of the "good fishing" label the Yukon government gives this location. Camping fee is $5.

LITTLE SALMON LODGE (private)
Kilometer 469.9 (Mile 292) Campbell Highway

LITTLE SALMON CAMPGROUND (Yukon government)
Kilometer 516.9 (Mile 312.9) Campbell Highway

This campground at the east end of Little Salmon Lake offers 12 campsites, drinking water, toilets, and a boat launch. The approach road to this one is narrow, curvy, and steep in places; perhaps not the best choice for big rigs or large travel trailers. Camping fee is $5.

FRENCHMAN'S LAKE CAMPGROUND (Yukon government)
Three kilometers (1.8 miles) on an access road that junctions with the
Campbell Highway at Kilometer 559.6 (Mile 338.8).

Fourteen campsites are located here, in a site which also offers drinking water, fire grates, toilets, a boat launch, and fair to good fishing for lake trout and grayling. Camping fee is $5.

NUNATAK CAMPGROUND (Yukon government)
Fifteen kilometers (9.3 miles) on the same access road as Frenchman's
Lake Campground, which junctions with the Campbell Highway at
Kilometer 559.6 (Mile 338.8).

Thirteen campsites, drinking water, fire grates, kitchen shelter, and a boat launch are located at this rather isolated, and therefore less visited, wayside. It is listed by the Yukon government as a good fishing site.

At Kilometer 572.6 (Mile 355.8), the Campbell Highway junctions with the Klondike Highway near the community of Carmacks. For camping opportunities there, see page 76. At Carmacks, incidentally, it is a good idea to gas up your vehicle. No matter which way you are traveling—southeast to Watson Lake, north to Dawson City, or south to Whitehorse—service stations are infrequent.

The Canol Road (Yukon Highway 6)

This highway is another World War II veteran, but there has been very little development along the way since the war ended. Constructed as an oil pipeline route from Norman Wells in the Northwest Territories to Whitehorse, the 472-kilometer (295-mile) road today is basically a frontier supply route maintained to minimum standards.

The name "Canol" derives from its original designation as the "Canadian Oil Road." The road actually has two halves, which divide roughly at the community of Ross River. South of its junction with the Campbell Highway at Kilometer 224.4 (Mile 139.4), the route is called the South Canol. North of Ross River it is called, of course, the North Canol. Both halves are narrow and curvy with a lot of ups and downs. Big rigs and large travel trailers might have problems; only the hardy should drive this road.

The South Canol, although rough in many places, is decidedly better than its northern counterpart. There are only three public (and no private) campgrounds along the north and south sections. Services are available only at Ross River where the road junctions with the Campbell Highway.

If you are game, it is a cinch you will be the only one in your camping club or neighborhood who can say, "I camped the Canol." Here are the campgrounds along the way.

NISUTLIN RIVER CAMPGROUND (Yukon government)
Kilometer 67.5 (Mile 41.2) Canol Road

This is an unofficial, bare-bones campground with 4 tables, 4 fire pits, and 2 toilets; plus a million-dollar riverside setting. The odds are overwhelming that no one will come around to collect a campground fee from you here.

QUIET LAKE CAMPGROUND (Yukon government)
Kilometer 98.7 (Mile 60) Canol Road

Eight campsites are located on this lake rated as good fishing for lake trout, grayling, and northern pike. A boat launch is located here, as this is a popular putting-in point for canoeists and kayakers who want to paddle the Big Salmon River. Camping fee is $5.

Although not located on the Canol Road, the Yukon government Lapie Canyon Campground (at Kilometer 375 on the Campbell Highway) can be accessed just 11 kilometers (6.8 miles) west of the junction of the South Canol Road and Campbell Highway. For details about this superior campground see page 81.

DRAGON LAKE CAMPGROUND (Yukon government)
Kilometer 333.7 (Mile 203) North Canol Road

Another bare-bones unofficial facility with camping area and toilet. There is a boat launch at the site.

At Kilometer 472.4 (Mile 295), you come to the Yukon Territory-Northwest Territories border. The road continued on from here in the old days, but is now grown over. Only all-terrain vehicles can negotiate what is left of the route now. It is time to turn around and come back.

The Dempster Highway (Yukon Highway 5)

This is it—the ultimate vacation route. The Dempster runs all the way to Inuvik, Northwest Territories, on the Mackenzie Delta, which drains into the Arctic Ocean. You can not drive on the connected highways of North America any farther north than this. (The Dalton Highway to Prudhoe Bay

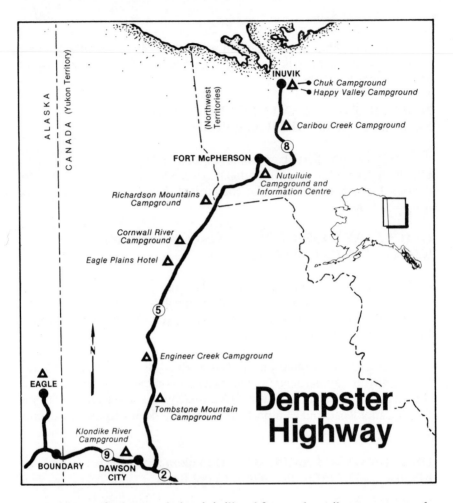

in Alaska goes farther north, but it is illegal for any but oil company supply trucks to drive the Dalton Highway much beyond the Arctic Circle.)

The Dempster is gravel and special precautions are advised: take extra gas and oil, extra spare tires, and extra fan belts. Extra food is also a must, and of course you should carry a first-aid kit and tools. Services, and even fellow travelers, are few and far between. All this sounds rather ominous, but the road is really quite negotiable. Northern travel veterans compare it to the Alaska Highway of perhaps a decade ago.

The rewards of travel above the Arctic Circle are enormous. Horizons of rolling hills covered with brilliant wildflowers are breathtaking, and so is the sight of caribou herds ranging across the endless tundra. The Dempster Highway begins at a junction with the Klondike Highway about 25 miles south of Dawson City. It ends some 450 miles later on the river delta which drains to the Beaufort Sea.

Following are the campgrounds along this fantastic journey.

TOMBSTONE MOUNTAIN CAMPGROUND (Yukon government)
Kilometer 74.5 (Mile 435.1) Dempster Highway

This is a pretty big campground considering its relative isolation. Twenty-one campsites are located here, along with fire grates, tables, and toilets. There is no developed water source but government bulletins advise the water from the nearby North Klondike River is safe to drink if boiled. A hiking trail takes off from the campground. Camping fee is $5.

ENGINEER CREEK CAMPGROUND (Yukon government)
Kilometer 195 (Mile 121.6) Dempster Highway

Another ample camping place, this wayside contains 23 campsites plus toilets, kitchen shelter, and group fire pit in a wooded streamside setting. There is no water well, and the water from Engineer Creek looks a bit orange, but the Yukon government says it is OK to drink if you boil it. Camping fee is $5.

EAGLE PLAINS HOTEL (private)
Kilometer 371.7 (Mile 231) Dempster Highway

Whether or not you overnight at the campground here, fill your fuel tanks. This (and the community of Fort McPherson just off the Dempster about 110 miles farther north) is the only service and supply station between the road's beginning and Inuvik at the highway's end.

CORNWALL RIVER CAMPGROUND (Yukon government)
Kilometer 448 (Mile 273) Dempster Highway

This is a brand-new wayside with spaces for 20 RVs. On-site are picnic tables, fire grates, and toilets. Camping fee is $5.

RICHARDSON MOUNTAINS CAMPGROUND (Yukon
government)
Kilometer 465 (Mile 288.8) Dempster Highway

Thirteen campsites are located here at the last Yukon government campground along this road. Facilities include tables, fire grates, toilets, but no water. There is a very satisfying view of the Richardson Mountains. Camping fee is $5. A couple of miles farther up the highway you will cross the pass that marks the Continental Divide in this range. West-flowing water drains to the Pacific Ocean; east-heading water ends up in the Arctic Ocean.

NUTUILUIE CAMPGROUND AND INFORMATION CENTRE
(Northwest Territories government)
Kilometer 543 (Mile 339) Dempster Highway

You are in the Northwest Territories now, so adjust your clocks and watches forward one hour to Mountain time. (Noon in the Yukon Territory is 1:00 P.M. in the Northwest Territories. The campground is located in a wooded setting on the Fort McPherson side of the Peel River, near the river ferry landing. It has 20 sites plus drinking water and toilets. Camping fee is $5.

CARIBOU CREEK CAMPGROUND (Northwest Territories government)
Kilometer 429 (Mile 690) Dempster Highway

Set in a wooded valley among tall (for the Northwest Territories) trees, Caribou Creek Campground has approximately 24 campsites plus firewood and grates, tables, and toilets. It has no well but water from the creek is OK to drink if it is boiled first. There is no charge for using this campground.

HAPPY VALLEY CAMPGROUND (city of Inuvik)
Located at the community of Inuvik, Northwest Territories, Kilometer 726 (Mile 451) Dempster Highway.

Inuvik is the northern terminus of the Dempster Highway and offers full services for the highway traveler. This community is, in fact, the largest Canadian community north of the Arctic Circle.

Happy Valley Campground is located just a block from downtown on the east bank of the Mackenzie River and has spaces both for campers (20) and tenters (10). On-site also are water, fire grates, firewood, and toilets. There is a $5 camping fee.

CHUK CAMPGROUND (Northwest Territories government)
Located at the community of Inuvik, Northwest Territories, Kilometer 726 (Mile 451) Dempster Highway.

Chuk Campground, about 2 miles from town on Airport Road, has 20 camping spaces plus water, toilets, fire grates, and wood. This is a hilltop campsite, with a very worthwhile view of the Mackenzie delta. This site has another advantage. If the mosquitoes are out in force (which they sometimes are), the Chuk Campground can be largely free of the pests, especially if a breeze is blowing. A $5 camping fee is charged.

The Atlin and Tagish Roads
(Yukon Highway 7 and Yukon Highway 8)

As you drive the Alaska Highway south of Whitehorse and arrive at Jake's Corner (Kilometer 1392.5, Mile 866), you have an opportunity to choose from two delightful side trips. The southerly route is the Atlin Road, which leads some sixty miles to Atlin, British Columbia. The other route is the Tagish Road; it heads southwesterly to Carcross on the Klondike Highway. Both roads are gravel but are usually in very drivable condition. If it has been raining, be cautious of slick surfacing. Both roads offer highly satisfying, off-beat views of lake, stream, and mountain country.

There are two campgrounds located on the Atlin Road.

SNAFU LAKE CAMPGROUND (Yukon government)
Located 26.4 kilometers (17 miles) south of the junction with the Alaska Highway.

Four campsites with tables, firegrates, and toilets are located here in a wooded setting. There is no developed water system but the lake water is OK to drink if you boil it. The Yukon government rates this site good fishing, especially for pike. Camping fee is $5.

TARFU LAKE CAMPGROUND (Yukon government)
Kilometer 32.6 (Mile 22) from the Alaska Highway junction.

Tarfu Lake Campground offers 4 campsites with the same good prospects for angling as Snafu Lake. There is no well but water from the lake is drinkable if boiled. Tables, firegrates, and toilets are located on-site. Camping fee is $5.

At the road's end the community of Atlin provides a public campground at the north end of the town. On Warm Bay Road, the privately operated Pine Creek Campground provides additional space for tenters and RV travelers.

Two public campgrounds are located along the Tagish Road.

TAGISH BRIDGE CAMPGROUND (Yukon government)
Kilometer 21 (Mile 13) Tagish Road.

Near the community of Tagish, the Tagish Bridge Campground is situated on the Six Mile River between Marsh Lake to the north and Tagish Lake to the south. More than 24 campsites are located there along with drinking water, tables, fire grates, picnic area, kids' playground, kitchen shelter, and toilets. To accommodate the good fishing in the area there is a fish filleting table and boat launch. Only a short distance farther, in the village of Tagish, additional government camping sites have been located.

At the road's end, where the Tagish junctions with the Klondike Highway at Carcross, a side road leads to Carcross Community Campground where 12 campsites have been established. There is no water supply on the grounds.

From Carcross you may, if you wish, drive the Klondike Highway about fifty kilometers (thirty miles) north to a junction with the Alaska Highway just south of Whitehorse.

Alaska's Major Highways

You finally made it: The sign at Mile 1221.8 Alaska Highway says Welcome to Alaska. Whether your route to this point was an all-Canadian road route or a combination of the Alaska Marine Highway and British Columbia-Yukon Territory roads, it is exciting to be on the verge of exploring new terrain.

You are now in the region that Alaskans call the Interior. This is the land of gold and sourdoughs. It is beautiful country, with miles and miles of heavily forested rolling hills. The region abounds with wildlife: moose, caribou, grizzly bears, wolves, and scores of smaller species. It is warm and balmy in the summertime, but bitterly cold in the winter. Temperatures can get down to minus eighty degrees and colder in December, January, and February.

You are going to love vacationing in the Great Land. Fairbanks, about three hundred miles to the north, is the hub city of the region as well as the second largest community in Alaska. Mount McKinley, at 20,320 feet the highest peak in North America, is located in the Interior surrounded by game-filled Denali National Park and Preserve.

The border station here is officially called Port Alcan, though there is not a seagoing vessel within hundreds of miles. The United States Customs and Immigration Service offices are open twenty-four hours a day year-round. It is mandatory for you to stop here for clearance to reenter the United States. Set your clocks and watches back one hour from Pacific to Alaska time: noon in the Yukon Territory becomes 11:00 A.M. in Alaska.

Alaska Highway (Alaska Highway 2)

Following are campground facilities on the Alaska Highway from the border to Fairbanks.

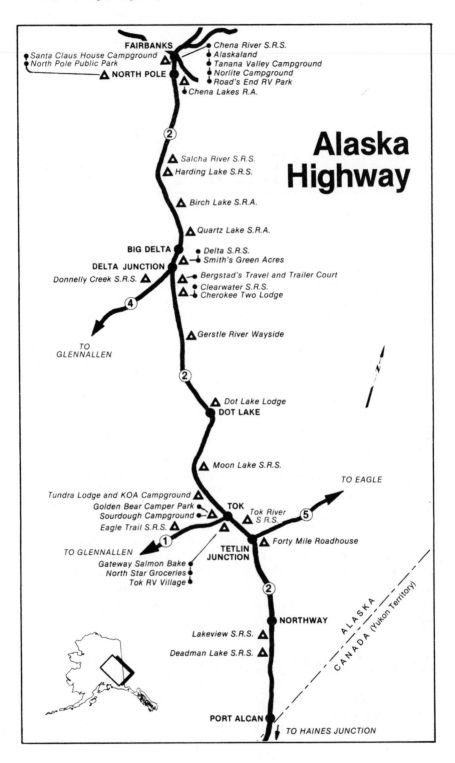

FAIRBANKS
Chena River S.R.S.
Santa Claus House Campground
North Pole Public Park
Alaskaland
Tanana Valley Campground
NORTH POLE
Norlite Campground
Road's End RV Park
Chena Lakes R.A.

2

Salcha River S.R.S.
Harding Lake S.R.S.

Birch Lake S.R.A.

Quartz Lake S.R.A.

BIG DELTA
Delta S.R.S.
DELTA JUNCTION
Smith's Green Acres
Donnelly Creek S.R.S.
Bergstad's Travel and Trailer Court
Clearwater S.R.S.
Cherokee Two Lodge

4

Gerstle River Wayside

TO
GLENNALLEN

2

Dot Lake Lodge
DOT LAKE

Moon Lake S.R.S.

Alaska Highway

TO EAGLE

Tundra Lodge and KOA Campground
Golden Bear Camper Park
TOK
Sourdough Campground
Tok River S.R.S.
Eagle Trail S.R.S.
5

1
Forty Mile Roadhouse

TO GLENNALLEN
TETLIN JUNCTION
Gateway Salmon Bake
North Star Groceries
Tok RV Village

2

NORTHWAY
Lakeview S.R.S.
Deadman Lake S.R.S.

A L A S K A
C A N A D A (Yukon Territory)

PORT ALCAN
TO HAINES JUNCTION

Note: Some out-of-date maps show Gardiner Creek campground about twenty-five miles northwest of the border crossing. Do not bother looking for it. It is closed—and a good thing, too. It was one of Alaska's least attractive camping facilities.

DEADMAN LAKE STATE RECREATION SITE (Alaska State Parks)
Mile 1249 Alaska Highway

This facility offers the visitor a pleasant camping introduction to Alaska. Canoeing is popular here. There is a boat launch ramp (though it is unsurfaced and sometimes muddy), and the lake contains northern pike. Swimming is also popular. There are 16 camping units located on the 20-acre site, but there is no approved drinking water source. Camping limit is 15 days. There is no charge here or at other Alaska State Parks campgrounds.

This is permafrost country. This means the ground is frozen solid and never thaws, except for the top several inches during summertime. This produces some fascinating effects. Along the sometimes rough entranceway leading into the campground, the tree roots next to the road have settled. As a result, the trees lean in on each side, forming an arch over the road.

Even more curious, the original concrete fireplaces had gradually descended as much as 15 inches below the ground's surface due to thawing of the permafrost by heat from cooking fires and the sun. The cooking facilities were recently replaced. Permafrost has created an opposite effect on the pit toilets here. Frost action actually thrusts the toilet vault beneath each privy upward a few inches every year or so. As a result, the state occasionally has to add a new step to the stairs in front of each outhouse.

LAKEVIEW STATE RECREATION SITE (Alaska State Parks)
Mile 1256 Alaska Highway

Located about 35 miles from the border in a very attractive setting, Lakeview SRS is relatively undeveloped. The unit contains 8 camping sites, no water wells, and the camping limit is 15 days. The road into the site might be a problem for large RVs because of its location on a rather steep, sloping hillside; it is not recommended for trailers. Pickup campers, vans, and tenters should do fine. Attractions include a boat launch, canoeing, fishing, waterfowl watching, and swimming on scenic Yarger Lake.

At Mile 1302, the Alaska Highway junctions with the Taylor Highway. For campgrounds along this route see pages 131–134.

FORTY MILE ROADHOUSE (private)
Mile 1302 Alaska Highway

TOK RIVER STATE RECREATION SITE (Alaska State Parks)
Mile 1309 Alaska Highway

This wayside, located on the banks of the Tok (rhymes with joke) River about 4 miles south of the town of Tok, has recently undergone considerable expansion and upgrading. It now contains 60 parking spaces, 25 RV units, 5 tent sites, picnic shelter and facilities, drinking water, toilets, a handicap-access interpretative nature trail, and information about Alaska parks statewide. There is a gravel boat ramp to the stream. Caution: Be careful in or around this river; it is swift and can be dangerous. Camping limit is 15 days.

Note: When you drive through Tok, be sure to visit the information center at Mile 1314 where coffee, travel suggestions, and road reports are dispensed daily. An exhibit of mounted Alaska wild animals at the center is especially noteworthy. Among the critters on display there: the seventh highest rated Dall mountain sheep in the record books, musk-ox, polar and brown bears, mounted walrus head and cape, moose, caribou, and full-mount wolves.

At Mile 1314 the Alaska Highway junctions with the Tok Cutoff/ Glenn Highway to Anchorage. For a listing of all the campgrounds along this route see pages 101–109. The following six campgrounds, along with the Tok River SRS previously listed, serve Tok visitors. Note that several are on the Tok Cutoff/Glenn Highway, not the Alaska Highway.

GATEWAY SALMON BAKE (private)
Mile 1313 Alaska Highway

NORTH STAR GROCERIES (private)
Mile 1313.3 Alaska Highway

TOK RV VILLAGE (private)
Mile 1313.4 Alaska Highway

GOLDEN BEAR CAMPER PARK (private)
Located approximately .3 mile west of junction on Tok Cutoff/Glenn Highway.

SOURDOUGH CAMPGROUND (private)
Located approximately 1.7 miles west of junction on Tok Cutoff/Glenn Highway.

EAGLE TRAIL STATE RECREATION SITE (Alaska State Parks)
Located approximately 15.7 miles west of junction on Tok Cutoff/
Glenn Highway.

If the Tok River state campground is full and you prefer public to
private overnight facilities, this wayside is an excellent choice. Forty
camping units are located here on a 640-acre site. Camping spaces are
separated from one another among spruce and birch stands. In mid-July and
August there are profusions of fireweed and other wildflowers in the area.
Four picnic sites and a generously sized shelter are available. There is on-site
water for drinking from a hand pump, but no water recreation. Toilets are
concrete-vault type, much pleasanter than the outhouses you frequently find
in northern campgrounds.

Access to the campground is designed for large rigs. A portion of the
historic sourdough trail to Eagle is located on these grounds and nearly a
mile of hiking trail is signed to help you enjoy it. There is some fishing for
grayling at the mouth of Clearwater Creek where it empties into the Tok
River. Camping limit is 15 days.

TUNDRA LODGE and KOA CAMPGROUND (private)
Mile 1315 Alaska Highway

MOON LAKE STATE RECREATION SITE (Alaska State Parks)
Mile 1332 Alaska Highway

Eighteen miles west of Tok is this 22-acre wayside containing 15
camping units and 15 picnic sites. It is the last public campground until you
get to the Delta Junction area some 80-plus miles down the road. Drinking
water is available at Moon Lake, as are handicap-access toilets, picnic sites,
and the opportunity for swimming and canoeing. Fishing is not very
productive here. There is an unsurfaced boat launch leading into the lake, an
old oxbow of the nearby Tanana River. The road leading into the area
descends at a rate that indicates caution (although no real problem) for
vehicles pulling trailers. Camping limit is 15 days.

DOT LAKE (community)
Mile 1361.5 Alaska Highway

DOT LAKE LODGE (private)
Mile 1361.5 Alaska Highway

GERSTLE RIVER WAYSIDE (State Department of Highways)
Mile 1393 Alaska Highway

This is not really a campground but it is OK to overnight here. There are toilets, but no drinking water.

CHEROKEE TWO 'LODGE' (private)
Mile 1412.5 Alaska Highway

CLEARWATER STATE RECREATION SITE (Alaska State Parks)
Access road at Mile 1415 Alaska Highway

This campground would be easy to miss—but should not be. The site is about 8 miles northeast of the Alaska Highway on Remington Road. There are 18 camping units on this 27-acre site, which also provides water and toilet facilities.

The campground lies adjacent to Clearwater Creek, a beautiful clear stream, which offers fishing for grayling and whitefish, plus boating and canoeing. It also provides access to the Tanana and Goodpaster rivers. Since the area is located some distance from the highway the campground is usually quiet and uncrowded. In the fall especially you may see bison in the area. If you do, keep your distance. The huge, shaggy creatures are not domestic animals! Lodging, gas, and groceries are located nearby. Camping limit is 15 days.

When you get ready to leave the campground, if you want to bypass Delta Junction you can head westerly on the Jack Warren Road to rejoin the main highway just north of the city.

BERGSTAD'S TRAVEL AND TRAILER COURT (private)
Mile 1420.9 Alaska Highway

DONNELLY CREEK STATE RECREATION SITE (state of Alaska)
Mile 238 Richardson Highway

Note that Donnelly Creek SRS is on the Richardson, not the Alaska, Highway. To get to this campsite, Alaska Highway travelers drive to Delta Junction (Mile 1422) then head about 28 miles south down the Richardson Highway to Mile 238 on that road.

This is a pleasant site, timbered with stands of relatively short growth. The wind blows often and hard, however, so it is probably not the best choice for a tent camp. The view of some of the tallest peaks in the Alaska Range is spectacular. There is fishing for grayling in the area and this is also country where the buffalo roam. Twelve camping units are located here on a 42-acre site with picnic facilities, drinking water, and toilets. Camping limit is 15 days.

**Special Note Regarding Milepost Markings,
Delta Junction to Fairbanks**

When you get to Delta Junction and Mile 1422 you are officially at the end of the Alaska Highway, and the mileposts no longer measure distance from Dawson Creek, British Columbia, where the Alaska Highway begins. From this point to Fairbanks you are really on the Richardson Highway.

Frequently, however, both visitors and even Alaskans consider Fairbanks to be the northernmost point of the Alaska Highway. Because of this, and because the state's official state highway numbering system shows state highway 2 extending from the border to Fairbanks, we are treating the highway from Delta Junction to Fairbanks as a continuation of the Alaska Highway.

The mileposts beside the road, however, measure mileage from Valdez on the southcentral coast of Alaska, not from Dawson Creek, British Columbia. This is a richly historical route. The Richardson had its origins in Alaska's frontier days when the road served as a horse and dog team trail from tidewater to the goldfields around Fairbanks. For more information and a listing of campgrounds along the Richardson between Valdez and Delta Junction, see pages 118–123.

DELTA STATE RECREATION SITE (Alaska State Parks)
Mile 267.1 Richardson Highway

This is a former Bureau of Land Management campground now operated by the state of Alaska. Located 1.5 miles north of the junction of the Alaska and Richardson highways, it is a clean, relatively large facility offering 22 camping units plus picnic sites, water, and toilets. Commercial showers and laundry facilities are available in the vicinity, though not in the campground itself. The site is next to an airstrip; do not be surprised if fly-in campers drop down from the sky to join you.

This is also a convenient campground for travelers who want to spend some time at the Big Delta State Historical Park located at Mile 274.5 Richardson Highway. The historical park has no camping facilities but does contain the remains of an old United States Signal Corps telegraph station, a restored roadhouse at the crossing of the Tanana River and the Valdez-Fairbanks trail, and a small museum. Picnic sites, handicap-access toilets, and a self-guided tour are also features of the park.

SMITH'S GREEN ACRES (private)
Mile 268 Richardson Highway

BIRCH LAKE STATE RECREATION AREA
Access via a gravel road that junctions with the Richardson Highway at Mile 306.

To reach this small recreation site, turn left about .25 mile down the access road. If you come to the United States Air Force Recreation Camp, you have driven too far. A toilet and parking lot (where informal RV camping is allowed) are the only services provided here. It is, however, a pleasant site for picnicking, swimming, fishing, and boating.

QUARTZ LAKE STATE RECREATION AREA (Alaska State Parks)
A three-mile access road junctions with the Richardson Highway at Mile 277.8.

This 600-acre recreation area actually contains two lakes: Lost Lake (which is easy to find) and Quartz Lake. To reach Lost Lake from the access road turn left at the intersection about 2.5 miles in from the highway; to reach Quartz Lake (which has almost all of the area's 16 campsites) keep going straight another 1/3 mile.

The grounds here are gently rolling hills, with several good vantage points for viewing the Alaska Range. Wildlife watching is popular, especially at seldom-crowded Lost Lake. Fishing is good in Quartz (but not Lost) Lake for stocked rainbows and silver salmon. For this reason it is often crowded, particularly on weekends and holidays. The trans-Alaska pipeline can be seen from the access road into Quartz Lake.

Improvements include 16 camping sites, a parking lot where over-nighting is also allowed, boat launch, drinking water, handicap-access toilets, picnic site with shelter, and a sandy beach. Camping limit is 15 days.

HARDING LAKE STATE RECREATION AREA (Alaska State Parks)
Mile 169 Richardson Highway

This popular area is located at the southwest corner of one of Interior Alaska's largest bodies of water. Eighty-nine camping units are located here. The lake boasts one of the relatively few paved boat launches in the area plus a sand and gravel swimming beach. (The water is shallow. You can wade out 100 yards and still be in water only waist deep.) There are changing rooms, 52 picnic units, toilets, fresh water sources and—another rarity in Alaska public campgrounds—a dump station. Canoeing and fishing are also popular here. On-shore there are a baseball field, volleyball court, horseshoe pits, and a group campfire area. Camping limit is 15 days.

SALCHA RIVER STATE RECREATION SITE (Alaska State Parks)
Mile 323.3 Richardson Highway

Just a couple of miles past the Harding River recreation area is this smaller (62 acres) wayside with handicap-access toilets, picnic facilities, boat launch, and swimming/fishing waters. There are no developed camping spaces but informal overnight camping is allowed on a gravel bar at the site. The state describes the angling for grayling, king and silver salmon as excellent.

CHENA LAKES RECREATION AREA (Fairbanks North Star
Borough)
Access is via northbound Laurence Road at Mile 346.7 Richardson Highway, 1 mile south of North Pole.

Not to be confused with the Chena River SRS in Fairbanks, nor with the Chena River SRA located on the Chena Hot Springs Road, this particular site is a borough (county) park created in conjunction with a United States Corps of Engineers dam and flood control project. It is a sprawling lake-oriented 2,178-acre site with 81 campsites, water pumps, toilet facilities, dump station, numerous picnic areas with covered pavilions, swimming beaches; even such amenities as volleyball courts, children's playground, and at least one island with camping/picnic facilities.

Not surprisingly for such a state-of-the-art park, there is a charge for overnighting here. But it is only $5 per night; well worth the price. In the man-made, 259-acre Chena Lake, angling is for stocked rainbow and salmon. The Chena River offers grayling, northern pike, whitefish, and burbot. There is a network of trails for hiking and biking in the park. Keep a sharp eye out and you may see moose, especially cows with calves. Also in the area are beavers, muskrat, and foxes.

SANTA CLAUS HOUSE CAMPGROUND (private)
Mile 349.1 Richardson Highway

Free camping here for self-contained RVs. Camping area adjoins Santa Claus House gift shop in the city of North Pole. You can arrange for Christmas cards postmarked *North Pole, Alaska*, to be sent from here just before Christmas.

NORTH POLE PUBLIC PARK (city of North Pole)
Located on 5th Avenue.

This is a small area with paved parking for RVs and trailers plus tent sites in adjoining woods for tenters. There is no fee.

ROAD'S END RV PARK (private)
Mile 356 Richardson Highway

CHENA RIVER STATE RECREATION SITE (Alaska State Parks)
Off Airport Road at University Avenue on the Chena River.

This is the most convenient camping site for visitors to Fairbanks. The campground is an in-town, newly reopened state-operated campground with 69 campsites, running water, handicap-access rest room facilities, boat launch, volleyball court, trails, and day-use picnic area with shelter.

Camping use is limited to 4 days. A dump station is located in the recreation site and city dump station is located on 2nd Avenue.

ALASKALAND (city of Fairbanks)
Located at 410 Cushman.

Alaskaland is the state's pioneer theme park: dozens of acres of historic log cabins and buildings, museum, sternwheel riverboat, rides, salmon bake, re-created Native village, theater, and, of course, a frontier saloon. RV parking is allowed in the spacious parking lot. Daily fee is $5; limit is 5 nights.

A free city dump station is located on 2nd Avenue about 1 block from the service entrance to Alaskaland. Potable water is also available.

TANANA VALLEY CAMPGROUND (private)
Mile 2 College Road

Located at the Tanana Valley Fairgrounds (where horse shows and other local happenings are frequently in progress), this campground offers space for RVs and tenters. On-site are fireplaces and firewood, showers, laundry, toilets, and dump station. No electric hookups.

NORLITE CAMPGROUND (private)
About 1/3 mile south of Airport Road on Peger Road.

CHENA RIVER STATE RECREATION AREA (Alaska State Parks)
See Steese Highway section, page 126.

In the Fairbanks area, the Richardson Highway junctions with the Steese and Elliott highways. For campgrounds along these routes see pages 126–129 and 129–130, respectively.

The Glenn Highway/Tok Cutoff
(Alaska Highway 1)

Let us back up a little bit. In the previous section of this chapter we listed campgrounds from the Alaska border through Tok to Fairbanks. However, when you have traveled the Alaska Highway through Canada, crossed the border into Alaska, and come to the community of Tok, you have two equally pleasurable travel options.

You can continue north on the Alaska and Richardson highways to Fairbanks, or you can head west on the Glenn Highway toward Anchorage.

You can not go wrong either way, but the Glenn is certainly a highway of varied sights and scenes. The sky-piercing Mentasta and Wrangell mountain ranges abut this route. The road dissects long, wide valleys of spruce-alder-birch forests. In the Matanuska and Susitna valleys your path explores Alaska's principal agricultural districts. When you arrive at Anchorage you may be surprised to learn you have come to one of the nation's most cosmopolitan communities, but with a distinctively Alaska flavor. Fishing opportunities are fair to excellent all along the way and the chances of seeing wild game are at least as good, probably better, along the Glenn as they are along any of the state's major highways.

The 325-mile-long highway is a paved, modern road, which technically is made up of three segments, all of which are known collectively these days as "the Glenn." From Tok to Gakona Junction, a distance of 125 miles, the road is actually the Tok Cutoff. From Gakona Junction to Glennallen (14 miles) the road is simultaneously a portion of the Richardson Highway. From Glennallen to Anchorage (189 miles) the route is that of the original Glenn Highway.

The mileposts along the highway are a little confusing. Along the old Tok Cutoff section they indicate the number of miles from Gakona Junction. When you are traveling the short Richardson Highway portion they show the mileage from Valdez. From Anchorage to Glennallen the numbers indicate distance from Anchorage. In order to orient the traveler to the milepost markers beside the road, we will show mileages that correspond to those markers. However, in order to indicate miles to or from Alaska's largest city, we will also indicate distance from Anchorage by showing this mileage in parentheses.

Since substantial numbers of travelers route themselves from Tok to Anchorage, we are listing campgrounds southwesterly along the same routing. The milepost numbers, therefore, get smaller the closer you get to Anchorage.

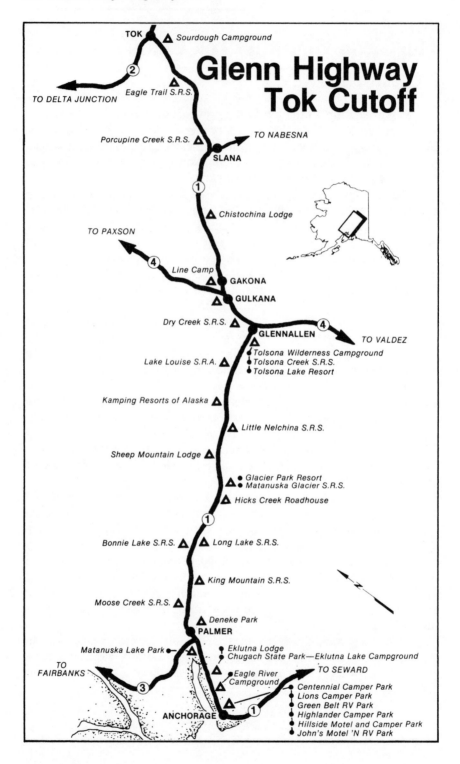

Glenn Highway Tok Cutoff

TOK

Sourdough Campground

TO DELTA JUNCTION

Eagle Trail S.R.S.

Porcupine Creek S.R.S.

TO NABESNA

SLANA

Chistochina Lodge

TO PAXSON

Line Camp

GAKONA

GULKANA

Dry Creek S.R.S.

GLENNALLEN

TO VALDEZ

Tolsona Wilderness Campground
Tolsona Creek S.R.S.
Tolsona Lake Resort

Lake Louise S.R.A.

Kamping Resorts of Alaska

Little Nelchina S.R.S.

Sheep Mountain Lodge

Glacier Park Resort
Matanuska Glacier S.R.S.

Hicks Creek Roadhouse

Bonnie Lake S.R.S.   Long Lake S.R.S.

King Mountain S.R.S.

Moose Creek S.R.S.

Deneke Park

PALMER

Matanuska Lake Park

Eklutna Lodge
Chugach State Park—Eklutna Lake Campground

TO
FAIRBANKS

Eagle River
Campground

TO SEWARD

Centennial Camper Park
Lions Camper Park
Green Belt RV Park
Highlander Camper Park
Hillside Motel and Camper Park
John's Motel 'N RV Park

ANCHORAGE

Following are campgrounds along this exciting road. (For a list of campgrounds in or close to Tok, but located on the Alaska Highway, see pages 94–95.)

SOURDOUGH CAMPGROUND (private)
Mile 122.8 Tok Cutoff (Mile 325.8 from Anchorage)

EAGLE TRAIL STATE RECREATION SITE (Alaska State Parks)
Mile 109.3 Tok Cutoff (Mile 312.3 Glenn Highway)

Forty camping units are located on this 640-acre campground, as are 4 picnic sites, generous-sized picnic shelter, ventilated concrete-vault toilets (much pleasanter than most outhouses you find in northern campgrounds), and a hand-pump well. Access is designed for large rigs; separate spaces around a large circular park area are set among stands of birch and spruce. In late July/August, there are profusions of fireweed and wildflowers. A portion of the historic sourdough trail to Eagle is located on these grounds and nearly a mile of hiking trail is signed to help you enjoy it. There is some fishing for grayling at the mouth of Clearwater Creek where it empties into the Tok River. There is a 15-day limit.

PORCUPINE CREEK STATE RECREATION SITE (Alaska State Parks)
Mile 64.2 Tok Cutoff (Mile 267 from Anchorage)

Located about .25 mile from the highway, this 12-unit campground is certainly not Alaska's biggest, but it is a pleasant, nicely situated area with a view of the Wrangell Mountains to the south and lots of room (240 acres) in which to roam. Individual camper spaces are set among spruce and willow trees around a large circular open area.

Like the Eagle Trail SRS 45 miles up the road, the open places burst into color as the summer season progresses; reddish purple fireweed is especially notable and picture worthy. Facilities include fireplaces, toilets, picnic tables, water, and trail. There is a 15-day limit.

CHISTOCHINA LODGE (private)
Mile 32.9 Tok Cutoff (Mile 235.8 from Anchorage)

LINE CAMP (private)
Mile .2 Tok Cutoff (Mile 203.2 from Anchorage)

At Gakona Junction (Mile 203 Glenn Highway), the Tok Cutoff/ Glenn Highway junctions with the northbound Richardson Highway. For a listing of campgrounds along the Richardson from Valdez to Delta Junction see pages 118–123. For Richardson campgrounds from Delta Junction to Fairbanks see pages 97–100.

For the next fourteen miles southbound, the Tok Cutoff/Glenn Highway and the Richardson Highway are all the same road.

GULKANA (community)
Mile 126.9 Richardson Highway (Mile 201 from Anchorage)

Camping is allowed on the banks of the Gulkana River. Signs in the area tell you where to pay daily camping fee.

DRY CREEK STATE RECREATION SITE (Alaska State Parks)
Mile 117.5 Richardson Highway (Mile 191 from Anchorage)

Five miles north of Glennallen, this 58-unit campground is scenically located in thick woods with nicely separated spaces—many of them pull-throughs. There is a separate walk-in tenters area. (A sign asks that you please pack out what you pack in.) On-site, too, are drinking water, picnic facilities, and toilets.

A small log cabin visitor center is located on the grounds but is not always open. Caution: The area can be "buggy" because of the black spruce forest. Bring along some insect repellent. Camping limit is 15 days.

Mile 189 from Anchorage is the southern end of the fourteen-mile stretch where the Glenn Highway/Tok Cutoff and Richardson are all the same road. The Glenn continues westerly to Anchorage at this point while the Richardson Highway veers southerly to Valdez. For a listing of campgrounds along that portion of the Richardson see pages 118–122.

TOLSONA WILDERNESS CAMPGROUND (private)
Mile 173 Glenn Highway

TOLSONA CREEK STATE RECREATION SITE (Alaska State Parks)
Mile 172.5 Glenn Highway

Ten camping units have been built at this wayside, which provides an adequate place for spending the night, but it is nothing spectacular. There is not much level land, and is not the best choice for big rigs or trailers. No water well is located on-site. Picnic facilities and toilet accommodations are available. There is some fishing, and a trail. There is a 15-day limit.

TOLSONA LAKE RESORT (private)
Mile 170.5 Glenn Highway

LAKE LOUISE STATE RECREATION AREA (Alaska State Parks)
Access road at Mile 159 Glenn Highway.

This parkland, located near the end of a 19-mile gravel access road, contains 21 campsites, picnic facilities, handicap-access toilets, and new boat launch. Fishing is productive here for grayling and lake trout. Some folks enjoy swimming in the lake waters as well as canoeing and kayaking. There is a 15-day limit.

The state campground is located off Mile 17 on the access road. A private campground facility, **Evergreen–the Lodge at Lake Louise**, is located at Mile 16.5.

KAMPING RESORTS OF ALASKA (private)
Mile 153 Glenn Highway

LITTLE NELCHINA STATE RECREATION SITE (Alaska State Parks)
Mile 137.4 Glenn Highway

A rather steep side road off the Glenn Highway provides access to this wayside on the shores of the Little Nelchina River. Eleven camping units have been located on 22 acres. One unique feature of this facility is the fossil beds upriver from the campgrounds. Picnic tables and fireplaces are on-site, but there is no developed water source, and the river water is too silty for drinking even if you boil it. Camping limit is 15 days.

SHEEP MOUNTAIN LODGE (private)
Mile 113.5 Glenn Highway

GLACIER PARK RESORT (private)
Mile 101 Glenn Highway

MATANUSKA GLACIER STATE RECREATION SITE (Alaska State Parks)
Mile 100 Glenn Highway

The view from any one of the 13 camping units within this recreation site is not particularly spectacular. However, from the very end of the road within the area the scenery and photographic opportunities are enormous. Too, hikers may take off from the road's end, traverse a ridgetop trail and, upon reaching a private road, gain access to the Matanuska Glacier itself. If you want to drive to the glacier's face, you must pay a daily fee to the private land owner (Glacier Park Resort, see above). Improvements at the state campground include water and picnic facilities. When hiking the glacier overlook, be very cautious near the edge of the bluff. There is a 15-day limit.

HICKS CREEK ROADHOUSE (private)
Mile 96.4 Glenn Highway

LONG LAKE STATE RECREATION SITE (Alaska State Parks)
Mile 85 Glenn Highway

The state maintains 8 camping units at this site, which provides easy open-space terrain for trailers. Canoeing and kayaking are popular here and fishing is considered good for grayling and burbot. Boats are easily launched from the sloping shore. Berry picking is also popular in the area. There is a chance you may see moose, bears, sheep (on the mountainsides), and other wildlife. Water and toilet facilities are available. There is a 15-day limit.

BONNIE LAKE STATE RECREATION SITE (Alaska State Parks)
Mile 83 Glenn Highway

This is an area of considerable beauty, located in a relatively high, rocky canyon. *If you are pulling a trailer, do not drive this road.* The 1.5-mile approach road off the Glenn Highway is steep, narrow, one-way in places, and slippery if it rains. (If it begins to sprinkle while you are there, you might wish to leave if your vehicle is not equipped with mud-grip tires.) Fishing for rainbow trout and grayling is considered pretty good in the lake. There is a launching ramp available in addition to the campground's 8 camping units, picnic facilities, toilets, and drinking water. Camping limit is 15 days.

KING MOUNTAIN STATE RECREATION SITE (Alaska State Parks)
Mile 76 Glenn Highway

This campground (formerly called Matanuska River Wayside) contains 22 camping units in 20 acres at the base of King Mountain. Water, toilets, and picnic shelter are available. The campground is situated among white spruce timber. The rocky Matanuska River rushes through the area at an enormous rate of speed. Early in the summer the water is relatively clear, but as the summer progresses the water becomes more and more milk colored from the silty runoff from melting glaciers upriver. There is a 15-day limit.

MOOSE CREEK STATE RECREATION SITE (Alaska State Parks)
Mile 54.5 Glenn Highway

This is a delightful area, located among tall birch and other leafy species in a level gravel-base valley floor just 6 miles north of Palmer. Moose Creek campground lies in a former coal mining area where even today veins of coal are exposed at the sides of the creek bed. Remains of an abandoned railroad right-of-way and of an old open-pit mine are also visible within the 40-acre campground.

Eight camping units are located here plus picnic accommodations including some covered tables. Fireplaces, handicap-access toilets, and a developed water source are also on site. Fishing for Dolly Varden is fair. Fossils may be found upstream in the water bed. Camping limit is 15 days.

KEPLER BRADLEY STATE RECREATION AREA (Alaska State Parks)
Mile 36.4 Glenn Highway

This is a lakes-oriented day-use area with interpretative displays, handicap-access trails, toilets, and good fishing. There are no camping spaces located here.

DENEKE PARK (city of Palmer)
Located at 435 South Denali Street, Palmer.

Tents, campers, motorhomes, and trailers may all be accommodated at this cozy municipal campground among stands of birch. City water is available and a dump station is on-site. Picnic tables, rest rooms, and hot showers are also available. There are no electric hookups. Cost is $4.50 per day. Fishing nearby is often productive for salmon, grayling, and trout.

About 6 miles west of the city of Palmer off Bogard Road is Finger Lake SRS (see George Parks Highway section, page 111).

At Mile 35 the Glenn Highway junctions with the George Parks Highway to Denali National Park and Preserve and Fairbanks. For a listing of campgrounds along this route see pages 109–118.

MATANUSKA LAKE PARK (private)
Located at junction of Glenn and George Parks highways.

EKLUTNA LODGE (private)
Mile 26.5 Glenn Highway

CHUGACH STATE PARK—EKLUTNA LAKE CAMPGROUND (Alaska State Parks)
Mile 26.5 Glenn Highway
EAGLE RIVER CAMPGROUND (Alaska State Parks)
Mile 12.6 Glenn Highway

Chugach State Park, not to be confused with the federally operated

Chugach National Forest nearby, was until recently the largest state park in the United States. It is 495,204 acres of pristine forests, snowcapped mountains, glistening lakes, plummeting waterfalls, and fish-filled streams.

Since it lies so near the heart of Alaska's largest city, it is well used and appreciated by Alaskan campers, hikers, fishermen, birders, wildlife viewers, wintertime skiers, even (in a restricted portion of the park) ATV and trail bike users. Throughout the park you may see moose, bears (exercise caution), Dall mountain sheep, foxes, and a rich abundance of bird life.

In spite of relatively heavy usage by Alaskans on weekends and on holidays, the park is seldom crowded any other time of the week.

Thunderbird Falls State Trail and Thunderbird Falls, which lie within the park boundaries, are probably overrated. The trail is a nice enough hike, and the grottolike falls are picturesque, but the surrounding hillsides are hazardous for climbing. Keep children off the inclines.

Eklutna Lake Campground is located on the shores of Eklutna Lake, about 10 miles easterly on the park road that leads from the Glenn Highway. Fifty spaces in a recently renovated camping area are located there, along with information kiosks, telescopes for spotting wildlife, handicap-access drinking water, picnic sites, handicap-access toilet facilities, and developed hiking trails (some of which are also handicap-accessible). Canoeing and boating are popular here, but there is no launch for large craft. Fishing is sometimes productive for rainbows and Dollys. Camping limit is 15 days.

Farther down the Glenn Highway at Mile 23.5, is Mirror Lake SRS. Do not let the appearance of numerous trailers and campers in the parking lot lead you to think you can overnight there. It is day-use only—and frequently a mob scene on sunny days. Nonetheless, it may well be worth a stop for its stocked, ample rainbow fishing; swimming from a small but pleasant bathing beach; canoeing and boating. (There is a paved double ramp.) It is, not surprisingly, most heavily used on weekends and holidays.

Eagle River Campground (access at Mile 12.6 Glenn Highway) is one of the most heavily utilized campgrounds in Alaska; primarily, of course, because it is so close to Anchorage, Alaska's largest city. Thirty-six camping units are located here; to get one you have to arrive well before evening. The setting is a pleasant one of birch and spruce trees.

Developed drinking water, handicap-access flush toilet facilities, and picnic tables and shelters are on-site. Canoeing and fishing are popular here as well. Camping at Eagle River Campground is limited to 4 days.

Other features of Chugach State Park include the Eagle River Visitor Center (access at Mile 13.6 Glenn Highway) where detailed trail and campground maps are available; an extensive and outstanding hillside trail system in the Upper O'Malley/Prospect and Upper Hoffman districts on the outskirts of Anchorage; McHugh Creek Picnic Area at Mile 111 Seward Highway; and Bird Creek Campground, Mile 101.5 Seward Highway. The latter two sites are described on pages 140–141.

CENTENNIAL CAMPER PARK (municipality of Anchorage)
Located at 8300 Glenn Highway south, off Glenn Highway at Muldoon Road.

This extensive campground (45 tent spaces, 85 for trailers and campers) includes city water, toilets, dump station, shower facilities (about which we have heard some complaints), trails, and freshwater lake fishing. A large variety of stores and service stations are located nearby. Moose and bears are sometimes seen in the vicinity. Camping limit is 7 days; $10 daily fee.

LIONS CAMPER PARK (municipality of Anchorage)
Located at 800 Boniface Parkway, 1 mile south off Glenn Highway.

This campground is located near stores, shops, and service facilities. The park in which the campground lies contains 360 acres of timbered city lands between 5th and 15th avenues. The area is also called Russian Jack Springs. Facilities include 10 tent spaces, 50 camper-trailer units, city water, trails, flush toilets, and a freshwater lake. There are no hookups or dump stations. Moose are sometimes seen in the area. Camping limit is 7 days; $10 daily fee.

GREEN BELT RV PARK (private)
Located at 5550 Old Seward Highway, phone 561-4610.

HIGHLANDER CAMPER PARK (private)
Located at 2704 Fairbanks Street, phone 277-2407.

HILLSIDE MOTEL AND CAMPER PARK (private)
Located at 2150 Gambell, phone 258-6006.

JOHN'S MOTEL 'N RV PARK (private)
Located at 3543 Mountain View Drive, phone 277-4332.

The George Parks Highway
(Alaska Highway 3)

Some folks assume the Parks Highway, as it is frequently called, derives its name from the fact that several of Alaska's most spectacular state and federal parklands lie along the highway route. Not so; the road was named for George Parks, a much revered Alaska territorial governor who served from 1925 to 1933. He died only recently, having passed the rich old age of

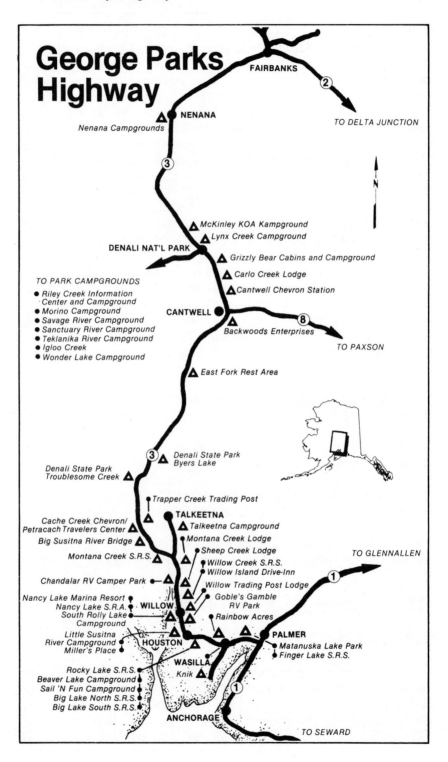

George Parks Highway

FAIRBANKS

TO DELTA JUNCTION

NENANA

Nenana Campgrounds

N

McKinley KOA Kampground

Lynx Creek Campground

DENALI NAT'L PARK

Grizzly Bear Cabins and Campground

Carlo Creek Lodge

Cantwell Chevron Station

TO PARK CAMPGROUNDS

- Riley Creek Information Center and Campground
- Morino Campground
- Savage River Campground
- Sanctuary River Campground
- Teklanika River Campground
- Igloo Creek
- Wonder Lake Campground

CANTWELL

Backwoods Enterprises

TO PAXSON

East Fork Rest Area

Denali State Park Byers Lake

Denali State Park Troublesome Creek

Trapper Creek Trading Post

TALKEETNA

Cache Creek Chevron/ Petracach Travelers Center

Talkeetna Campground

Big Susitna River Bridge

Montana Creek Lodge

Montana Creek S.R.S.

Sheep Creek Lodge

TO GLENNALLEN

Willow Creek S.R.S.

Willow Island Drive-Inn

Chandalar RV Camper Park

Willow Trading Post Lodge

Nancy Lake Marina Resort

Goble's Gamble RV Park

Nancy Lake S.R.A.

WILLOW

South Rolly Lake Campground

Rainbow Acres

Little Susitna River Campground

PALMER

Miller's Place

HOUSTON

Matanuska Lake Park

WASILLA

Finger Lake S.R.S.

Rocky Lake S.R.S.

Knik

Beaver Lake Campground

Sail 'N Fun Campground

Big Lake North S.R.S.

Big Lake South S.R.S.

ANCHORAGE

TO SEWARD

one hundred years.

If you have only limited time for touring/camping in Alaska, the George Parks Highway provides a generous offering of the best and most awesome that the North Country has to offer in the way of majestic mountains and wildlife. In spite of a few frost heaves here and there, this is probably the best maintained highway in the state.

The George Parks Highway connects Anchorage, Alaska's biggest city, with Fairbanks, the second largest. Actually, the first thirty-five miles out of Anchorage are on the Glenn Highway (Alaska Highway 1). The George Parks Highway begins at a junction located at approximately Mile 35 on the Glenn Highway. Please note that the George Parks Highway milepost numbers listed here and posted on the side of the road show distance from Anchorage, not from the start of the road.

For campground facilities along the Glenn Highway between Anchorage and the start of the George Parks Highway, and for campgrounds in or very near Anchorage, see pages 107–109.

MATANUSKA LAKE PARK (private)
Located at junction of the George Parks and Glenn highways.

FINGER LAKE STATE RECREATION SITE (Alaska State Parks)
At Mile 35.5 George Parks Highway, turn right on Trunk Road and drive to Bogard Road, then drive .7 mile on Bogard to campgound; or, at Mile 42.2 George Parks Highway turn right on Wasilla-Fishhook Road, follow it to Bogard Road, then drive 4 miles on Bogard Road to campground.

Finger Lake campground, 6 miles from Palmer and 50 miles from Anchorage, is an extremely popular year-round facility that offers ice-fishing in winter as well as angling for silver salmon, picnicking, and camping in the summer. Forty-one campsites plus picnic facilities, handicap-access toilets, pressure water system, and a boat launch are among its features. Camping limit is 7 days.

At Mile 42.2 George Parks Highway, you may turn south and drive thirteen miles to the community of Knik (pronounced kuh-Nick) on scenic Knik Lake. A private campground is located here.

RAINBOW ACRES (private)
Mile 49.4 George Parks Highway

BEAVER LAKE CAMPGROUND (private)
Mile 52.3 George Parks Highway

SAIL 'N FUN CAMPGROUND (private)
Mile 52.3 George Parks Highway

BIG LAKE NORTH STATE RECREATION SITE (Alaska State
** Parks)**
ROCKY LAKE STATE RECREATION SITE (Alaska State Parks)
BIG LAKE SOUTH STATE RECREATION SITE (Alaska State
** Parks)**
Located at Mile 52.3 George Parks Highway; southwesterly Big Lake
Road leads to these state and private campgrounds.

Big Lake is one of southcentral Alaska's favorite playgrounds. Miles of waterfront combined with good fishing for rainbow trout, lake trout, Dolly Varden, and burbot make this prime country for angling, sailing, canoeing, motorboating, and swimming.

If you have the choice, visit this area on weekdays, not weekends or holidays. You will find it far less crowded. Because of its popularity with Alaskans, and because quite a number of people maintain homes in the area, there are restaurants, marinas, and other commercial facilities available.

The campground at **Rocky Lake** has 10 camping units located on a water body that is smaller than Big Lake—but still quite pleasurable. There is a boat launch and good waters for canoeing and kayaking. Fishing is good for rainbow trout.

The land is level but the roadway through the recreation area is a bit narrow. Travelers with long trailers could experience some difficulty backing into a camping place. Camping limit is 7 days.

Big Lake North and **Big Lake South**, both state campgrounds, are located on the shores of the lake some 62 miles from Anchorage and 23 miles from Palmer. The north recreation site (formerly called Big Lake East) offers parking for 113 vehicles (essentially campsites for motorhomes, campers, and trailers), plus tent camping spaces, drinking water, interpretative displays, 2 boat launches, 22 picnic sites, and handicap-access toilets.

The south facility offers 13 units at the edge of a large parking pad. The view of the lake is much better here than at the north campground. Picnic sites, handicap-access toilets, drinking water, and surfaced launching pads are located at this area as well. Camping limit is 7 days at both sites.

About three and one-third miles down Big Lake Road from the George Parks Highway, the local Lions Club has provided a dump facility at the gas station located there.

LITTLE SUSITNA RIVER CAMPGROUND (city of Houston)
Mile 57.3 George Parks Highway

The city of Houston is proud of this campground, which contains 86 campsites, water wells, free firewood, rest rooms, and litter barrels. Visitor information is available from city hall next to the park. King and silver salmon fishing can be outstanding in the Little Susitna River. The kings arrive in late May and June and the silvers in July and August.

MILLER'S PLACE (private)
Mile 57.5 George Parks Highway

NANCY LAKE MARINA RESORT (private)
Mile 64.5 George Parks Highway

NANCY LAKE STATE RECREATION AREA (Alaska State Parks)
Mile 66.5 for access to Nancy Lake Campground and Mile 67.5 (the Nancy Lake Parkway) for balance of facilities.

Nancy Lake SRA is accessed from a somewhat poorly marked road at White's Crossing, Mile 66.5. The wayside offers 30 modern camping units situated in three cul-de-sacs. There are 30 picnic units separated from the camping area. A surfaced double boat ramp, handicap-access toilets, and good parking facilities are located here. Water, under pressure, is also available. The lake itself covers some 700 acres and is bordered by 24 miles of shoreline. Fishing is good for rainbow trout, silver salmon, Dolly Varden, whitefish, and burbot. Camping limit is 15 days.

Nancy Lake Canoe Trail begins at Mile 4.8 on the Nancy Lake Parkway. It offers 15 remote camping sites.

South Rolly Lake Campground is located at Mile 6.5 on the Nancy Lake Parkway and contains 98 camping units plus fireplaces, handicap-access toilets, and boat launch. Fishing for rainbows and swimming are popular activities at this site. Camping limit is 15 days.

While driving the parkway, plan to stop at the Tulik Nature Trail, which commences at Mile 3.5. The South Rolly Lake overlook and picnic site, located at Mile 6.2, is also worthwhile.

GOBLE'S GAMBLE RV PARK (private)
Mile 66.7 George Parks Highway

WILLOW TRADING POST LODGE (private)
Mile 69.5 George Parks Highway

WILLOW CREEK STATE RECREATION SITE (Alaska State Parks)
Mile 71.2 George Parks Highway then 1.3 miles east on Hatcher Pass Road.

Seventeen camping units are located on this 240-acre site. Picnicking and fishing are the principal attractions. There are handicap-access toilets, and the site has water from a well that is safe to drink, but it tastes awful. Better bring along your own. Do not drink water from the stream here. State officials warn of Giardia.

Note: Due to the meandering of the creek, the camping units here are split into three areas. If you find one area full, drive on to the next. Silver salmon, rainbow, and grayling are found in the waters here, as are Dolly Varden, chum salmon, kokanee, and pink salmon.

WILLOW ISLAND DRIVE-INN (private).
Mile 71.5 George Parks Highway

SHEEP CREEK LODGE (private)
Mile 88.2 George Parks Highway

CHANDALAR RV CAMPER PARK (private)
Mile 90.8 George Parks Highway

MONTANA CREEK STATE RECREATION SITE (Alaska State Parks)
Mile 96.5 George Parks Highway

There are no developed camping units here but the site does have parking for 92 vehicles including RVs. Facilities include handicap-access toilets, water, trails with handicap access, plus nearby fishing for king and silver salmon, grayling, Dolly Varden, and rainbows.

MONTANA CREEK LODGE (private)
Mile 96.5 George Parks Highway

TALKEETNA CAMPGROUND (public)
Located at Mile 98.7 George Parks Highway; the northbound Talkeetna Spur Road provides access.

Camper spaces, toilets, picnic facilities, and a boat launch are available at Christianson Lake.

BIG SUSITNA RIVER BRIDGE (State Department of Highways)
Mile 104.3 George Parks Highway

Parking area beside the bridge provides informal overnight camping. Toilets and water on-site.

CACHE CREEK CHEVRON/PETRACACH TRAVELERS CENTER (private)
Mile 114.8 George Parks Highway

TRAPPER CREEK TRADING POST (private)
Mile 115.5 George Parks Highway

DENALI STATE PARK (Alaska State Parks)
Mile 132.5 George Parks Highway

This 421,120-acre park is another of the jewels of the Alaska State Parks system. Features include wooded and alpine hiking trails (in the development stage, some are poorly marked at present), fabulous views of Mount McKinley and the surrounding peaks of the Alaska Range, fishing, picnicking, camping facilities, and a much-photographed Alaska Veterans Memorial (at Mile 147.2).

Troublesome Creek at Mile 137.2 is not really a campground but we spent a delightful night there a few years back, tenting beside the stream. The state actually maintains 2 trailheads, both with parking, toilets, and wells. Lower Troublesome Creek, which also includes a shelter, is accessed at Mile 137.2.

Byers Lake campground is another great overnight spot, especially if you are traveling by RV. (Tenters should use caution and store food well away from their camping spot. The bears in this area have been quite bold about inviting themselves to dinner.) The lake is closed to motor use, so canoeists and kayakers have a field day here. There are 66 campsites at the main camping area plus 5 remote sites across the lake.

EAST FORK REST AREA (State Department of Highways)
Mile 185.6 George Parks Highway

Overnight parking is OK at this gravel parking and picnic area surrounded by woods. Facilities include 24 picnic tables, fireplaces, toilets, and water well.

At Mile 210, the George Parks Highway junctions with the Denali Highway. For a listing of campgrounds along this route see pages 134–136.

BACKWOODS ENTERPRISES (private)
Mile 133.9 Denali Highway (about .20 mile east of the George Parks Highway on Denali Highway).

CANTWELL CHEVRON STATION (private)
Mile 210.4 George Parks Highway

CARLO CREEK LODGE (private)
Mile 223.9 George Parks Highway

GRIZZLY BEAR CABINS AND CAMPGROUND (private)
Mile 231.1 George Parks Highway

DENALI NATIONAL PARK AND PRESERVE, formerly MOUNT
McKINLEY NATIONAL PARK (National Park Service)
Boundary at Mile 231.3, park road entrance at Mile 237.3 George Parks
Highway.

Many consider visiting this park one of the premier outdoor experiences of the world. It is a park to be savored, never rushed through. Those who "do Denali" in a day or less might just as well pass it by. North America's highest peak, 20,320-foot Mount McKinley, is located here. Although it is never guaranteed, the chances of seeing lots of wildlife is probably better here than at any other park you can drive through in the country.

Grizzly and black bears, moose, caribou (in July, sometimes whole herds of them!), Dall mountain sheep, foxes, wolves (though abundant they are not frequently spotted), and an abundance of smaller creatures are the permanent residents that visitors come to see and photograph.

About the road: You do not simply "tour" this 91-mile route the way you do most places. In order to perpetuate Denali's superb wildlife viewing opportunities, the National Park Service has instituted a number of regulations for tenters and RV users.

First of all, in order to camp in the park you need to *apply in person* at Riley Creek information center (Mile .2 on the park road) for a campsite permit. These are granted on a first-come, first-served basis, and you cannot drive a vehicle beyond the Savage River checkpoint (Mile 12.8) without a permit. Any other travel beyond Savage River is via the free park service shuttle bus. If all camping spaces in the park are full on the day you are applying you can request a permit for the following day. There are several private campgrounds within easy driving distance of the park entrance. When you get a campsite permit, you may drive on the park road to the campsite you reserved—but no farther!

So how do you go about sightseeing in this fabulous park? Try the National Park Service shuttle buses. Each day, starting at 6:00 A.M. from Riley Creek, free shuttles operate up and down the park road, picking up passengers and dropping them off wherever the travelers desire. Stops are made, too, when wildlife comes in view.

Unlike the commercial (and frankly, more comfortable) tour buses, which also operate daily from the park hotel near the park entrance, the shuttle buses do not provide constantly guided narratives nor meals at the road's end. But they do offer all the various sights that the route has to offer: wildlife, dramatic and colorful geologic formations, and lens-filling views of

North America's highest peak *if* the mountain is not covered by clouds.

Following are the campgrounds maintained by the National Park Service along the park road.

Riley Creek Information Center and Campground, Mile .2, contains 102 camping spaces for tenters and RVers. Features include tap water, flush toilets, dump station, and nature trails nearby. Only gasoline station in the park is 1 mile farther up the road. Daily fee is $8.

Morino Campground, a walk-in-only facility, is located about **1/3 mile from the Denali Park railroad station at Mile 1.6.** There are 10 tent spaces and pit toilets. No charge.

Savage River Campground, Mile 12.8, has 29 camping units for tenters and RVers established here, the farthest point you can drive without a permit. Pit toilets, tap water on site. Daily fee is $8.

Sanctuary River Campground and Ranger Station, Mile 22, offers only 7 tent or RV camping units. Water at the source should be boiled before drinking. Pit toilets. No charge.

Teklanika River Campground, Mile 29.3, has 50 camping units for tenters and RVers. Tap water and pit toilets are located on-site. Daily fee is $8.

Igloo Creek, Mile 34.2, is another small camping area with 7 units for tenters only. Toilets are pit type. Water should be boiled. No charge.

Wonder Lake Campground, Mile 84.6, contains space for 20 tenters. Toilets are both flush and pit type. Water should be boiled or treated. This lake is well named; it is a wonder to behold! Dramatic, reflecting views of Mount McKinley can sometimes be seen and photographed across this water body. Camping fee is $8 daily.

There are no remote developed campsites in the park, however you can obtain a permit to backpack and camp in the park's backcountry. If you do, be extremely cautious around bears and other wildlife. Place food well away from camp.

Caution: The glacier-fed streams in the park can be swift and cold. Do not try to ford deep creeks. If you do your crossing in the early morning, before upstream glaciers begin their daily melt, the water will be considerably more shallow. Pick wide places in the streams to make your crossings. The water is, again, likely to be more shallow. Be sure to check in with the park service when you return.

LYNX CREEK CAMPGROUND (private)
Mile 238.6 George Parks Highway

McKINLEY KOA KAMPGROUND (private)
Mile 248.5 George Parks Highway

NENANA CAMPGROUNDS
Mile 304.7 George Parks Highway

The city of Nenana provided the following information regarding camping in this community: "At the present we have no [approved] campgrounds as they do not have toilet facilities. About one mile from the Visitors Center is a gravel pit where some tourists camp. It has no facilities. Some RVs stay right on the Visitors Center parking lot. A few have pitched tents around the *Taku Chief* river tug. There are three pullouts on, and just beyond, the bridge going toward Fairbanks. [And] there are three scenic pullouts [Mileposts 311, 317, 325]; self-contained RVs use them."

A private campground, The Last Resort, offers 15 spaces for self-contained RVs, but no tents. Check at the Tripod Gift Shop.

At Mile 358 the George Parks Highway junctions with Airport Way in Fairbanks. For a listing of public and private campgrounds in this city, see page 100.

The Richardson Highway
(Alaska Highway 4)

The Richardson Highway is both Alaska's oldest major highway and, according to many, its most scenic. The route begins at sea level in the mountain-rimmed community of Valdez (pronounced Val-DEEZ) and ends about 370 miles later at Fairbanks. For much of that distance it parallels the famed trans-Alaska oil pipeline, which originates on the Arctic coast and which provides 15 percent of America's crude oil. Although the highway ascends to high elevations very shortly after leaving Valdez and Keystone canyon, the grades are not overly steep. If your vehicle is not underpowered for the loads you are carrying or pulling you should not experience difficulty.

The Richardson had its beginnings during the last years of the nineteenth century, first as a gold stampeders trail, then as a wagon (and winter sled) road, ultimately as a modern highway. As the road nears its second century a few of the pioneer roadhouses still stand along the way as reminders of the era when overnight accommodations were spaced a day's horse or dog team travel apart.

The northernmost ninety-eight miles of the Richardson Highway from Delta Junction to Fairbanks are frequently, but erroneously, considered to be the final miles of the Alaska Highway. The mileposts alongside this portion of the road are Richardson Highway mileposts, and they indicate mileage distances from Valdez to Fairbanks, not Alaska Highway mileposts from Dawson Creek, British Columbia.

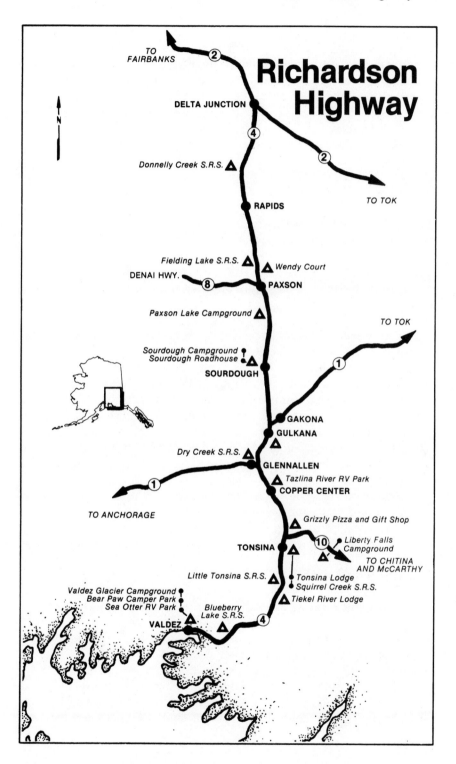

Richardson Highway

TO FAIRBANKS

② DELTA JUNCTION

④ ②

Donnelly Creek S.R.S. △

TO TOK

RAPIDS

Fielding Lake S.R.S. △ △ Wendy Court

DENAI HWY. ⑧ PAXSON

Paxson Lake Campground △

TO TOK

Sourdough Campground
Sourdough Roadhouse △
SOURDOUGH

①

GAKONA
GULKANA △

Dry Creek S.R.S. △

GLENNALLEN

△ Tazlina River RV Park
COPPER CENTER

① TO ANCHORAGE

△ Grizzly Pizza and Gift Shop

Liberty Falls
⑩ Campground
TONSINA △ △

TO CHITINA
AND McCARTHY

Little Tonsina S.R.S. △ Tonsina Lodge
Squirrel Creek S.R.S.

△ Tiekel River Lodge

Valdez Glacier Campground
Bear Paw Camper Park
Sea Otter RV Park
Blueberry
Lake S.R.S.
VALDEZ △ △ ④

The Richardson Highway mileposts were erected before the 1964 earthquake that destroyed the original city of Valdez. When the community was rebuilt on safer ground it was relocated four miles down the road, so the mileposts are four miles off as far as distance from the present city is concerned. Mile numbers listed here will correspond to the actual mileposts alongside the road.

Here are the campgrounds in Valdez and along this historic road.

BEAR PAW CAMPER PARK (private)
North Harbor Drive, in Valdez.

SEA OTTER RV PARK (private)
South Harbor Drive, in Valdez.

VALDEZ GLACIER CAMPGROUND (city of Valdez)
From Mile .6 Richardson Highway drive north at airport road for 2 miles.

This is one of Alaska's larger campgrounds, with 101 camping spaces plus water pumps, toilet facilities, picnic areas, but no dump station or hookups. Because there are so many things to do in this area, the wayside is considered by many to be a "destination" campground. Many travelers remain several days to sample fresh- and saltwater fishing, boating, and sightseeing. The road on which the campground is located begins at the original Valdez townsite and ends at the terminus of Valdez Glacier. Thousands of misguided gold seekers attempted to get to Interior goldfields during the gold rush days by hiking *over* this glacier—and many lost their lives in the attempt.

Black bears have been a frequent problem in this area. Do not leave garbage around your campsite. If you see any of the bruins, do not under any circumstances approach them.

There is no charge for using the campground. Camping limit is 15 days.

BLUEBERRY LAKE STATE RECREATION SITE (Alaska State Parks)
Loop road entrances at Miles 23 and 24 Richardson Highway.

The view of Keystone Canyon is spectacular here. The entire alpine setting of the recreation area makes it one of Alaska's most beautiful. Situated above timberline, the 9-space campground offers visitors the opportunity to study dwarfed plants and other flora typical of tundra environment. It can be blustery here if the wind is blowing. Birders take special note: This is a natural habitat for ptarmigan (Alaska's state bird) and flocks of several hundred are not uncommon in the area. Grayling fishing is also available. Facilities include sheltered picnic accommodations, handicap-access toilets, but no developed water source. Camping limit is 15 days.

Some out-of-date guides may show a campground at Worthington Glacier SRS at Mile 28.7. Although this roadside glacier is well worth a stop (and picnic facilities are located there), it is no longer an overnight camping site.

TIEKEL RIVER LODGE (private)
Mile 56 Richardson Highway

LITTLE TONSINA STATE RECREATION SITE (Alaska State Parks)
Mile 65 Richardson Highway

Here, where the rolling lands of the Copper River Valley break into the much more abrupt hill and mountain country of the Chugach Mountains, Little Tonsina recreation area offers 8 camping units in a 102-acre site. The weather is frequently sunnier here than in the coastal, maritime locale some 65 miles to the south. At times, however, the area is prone to rather high winds.

Fishing is considered good for grayling, Dolly Varden, and red salmon. Black bears sometimes wander through this area so if you are tenting leave your food in your vehicle, not your tent. If you are backpacking or biking, hang your food in a tree some distance from your camp and anyone else's. Fresh water, fireplaces, and toilets are on-site. Camping limit is 15 days.

TONSINA LODGE (private)
Mile 79 Richardson Highway

SQUIRREL CREEK STATE RECREATION SITE (Alaska State Parks)
Mile 79.5 Richardson Highway

Just off the highway, this campground is located on the banks of a small stream with rather barren cut banks on which some sagebrush is growing. The site contains 14 camping units in a 30-acre setting. The environment here is also very typical of the rest of the Copper River Valley, of which this is a part. The Alaska Department of Fish and Game reports fair angling for grayling and rainbows.

At Mile 82.5 the Richardson Highway junctions with the Edgerton Highway to Chitina and McCarthy. For a listing of campgrounds along this route see pages 161–162.

GRIZZLY PIZZA AND GIFT SHOP (private)
Mile 92 Richardson Highway

TAZLINA RIVER RV PARK (private)
Mile 110.5 Richardson Highway

At Mile 115 the Richardson Highway junctions with the Glenn Highway to Anchorage. For a listing of campgrounds along this route see pages 104–109.

DRY CREEK STATE RECREATION SITE (Alaska State Parks)
Mile 117.5 Richardson Highway

Five miles north of Glennallen, this 58-unit campground is scenically located in a heavily wooded locale. A number of the campground's 58 spaces are pull-throughs, and the site also contains a walk-in area for tenters. (A sign requests that you haul out whatever you haul in.) On-site are drinking water, picnic facilities, and toilets. A small log cabin visitor center is located there but is staffed on a limited basis. Caution: The area can be "buggy" because of the black spruce forest. Bring along some insect repellent. Camping limit is 15 days.

GULKANA (community)
Mile 126.9 Richardson Highway

Camping is allowed on the banks of the Gulkana River. Signs in the area tell you where to pay the daily camping fee.

At Mile 129 the Richardson Highway junctions with the Tok Cutoff/ Glenn Highway leading to Tok. For a listing of campgrounds along this route see pages 101–104.

SOURDOUGH CAMPGROUND (BLM)
Mile 147.6 Richardson Highway

This 20-unit wayside is located near the village of Sourdough, about 18 miles north of Gulkana. The campsite could be troublesome for large trailers. There are toilet facilities on-site but no developed drinking water sources. The Sourdough Creek, however, flows through the grounds and the water is drinkable after boiling. Best angling is for grayling. Camping limit is 7 days.

SOURDOUGH ROADHOUSE (private)
Mile 147.7 Richardson Highway

PAXSON LAKE CAMPGROUND (BLM)
Mile 175 Richardson Highway

A 1.5-mile gravel road leads to a 20-unit camping area at the lake. Some of the campsites located here are on a slope and could be awkward for RVs and trailers.

There is a canoe and boat launch accessed by a 200-foot boardwalk. Facilities include a well plus dump station. Fishing for trout and burbot can be productive in the lake. Camping limit is 7 days.

At Mile 186 the Richardson Highway junctions with the Denali Highway to Cantwell and Denali National Park and Preserve. For a listing of campgrounds along this route see pages 134–136.

WENDY COURT (private)
Mile 191.4 Richardson Highway

FIELDING LAKE STATE RECREATION SITE (Alaska State Parks)
Mile 200 Richardson Highway

This high-country (2,973 feet altitude), alpine campground presents a good view of the Alaska Range and contains 7 camping units, toilet facilities, but no developed water system. Located on a large lake on which there is often ice into July, the facility also has picnic tables and fireplaces. A commercial lodge and boat launch is nearby. Camping limit is 15 days.

DONNELLY CREEK STATE RECREATION SITE (state of Alaska)
Mile 238 Richardson Highway

This is a pleasant, seldom-crowded site, timbered with stands of relatively short growth. The wind blows often and hard, however, so it is probably not the best choice for a tent camp. The view of some of the tallest peaks in the Alaska Range is spectacular. There is fishing for grayling in the area, and this is country where the buffalo roam. Twelve camping units are located here on a 42-acre site with picnic facilities, drinking water, and toilets. Camping limit is 15 days.

Note: At Mile 266 in Delta Junction the Richardson Highway junctions with the Alaska Highway. The Alaska Highway from Dawson Creek, British Columbia, Canada, officially ends at this point and the Richardson continues on to Fairbanks. Most travelers, however, consider the leg from Delta Junction to Fairbanks to be a part of the Alaska Highway experience, and this is the way we have treated the road in this book. If you are driving from Valdez to Fairbanks, turn to page 97 in the Alaska Highway section for a continuation of the road and its campgrounds.

Interior
Alaska Highways

As we noted in the Alaska Highway section at the beginning of Chapter 4, the huge middle of the state that Alaskans call the Interior is a land of sourdoughs and gold. Incredibly, nearly a century after those first grizzled prospectors came searching over the region's hills, mountains, valleys, and water beds, the quest goes on. Outside of the larger communities and off the main highways this is still largely frontier country; men and women continue the sometimes frantic search in hopes of making the strike that will earn them millions.

It is along the roads described in this chapter that you will likely see them; these days operating dredges, bulldozers, or perhaps simply wielding a basic gold pan like the prospectors of yesteryear. You can try your hand at panning, too. (If you are on private land, get the owner's permission first. It is not considered friendly to work someone else's claim, and doing so can be downright dangerous.) Chances are you will not be able to pay for your vacation with your earnings but, who knows, you may just stumble across the fist-sized nugget that 18,327 other sourdoughs missed. Indeed, the world's largest nugget was only recently discovered in this area in an otherwise poorly rated claim.

As you tour the roads of the Interior, take time to stop at the infrequent roadhouses and eating spots to visit with the Alaskans you will meet there. These rugged folk are a vanishing breed. They are quiet people who treasure their relative isolation, especially during the winter months; men and women who take pride in providing much of their livelihood from skills with a rifle, an ax, and a small portion of fertile earth.

Homesteaders, prospectors, service station owners, trappers, roadhouse owners, perhaps even a few minerals geologists with Ph.D.'s; these are the residents of this region. Just knowing these people are "out there" gives many of us city-bound Alaskans pause to reflect with comfort on the frontier heritage that continues as the forty-ninth state prepares to close out the twentieth century.

Here, then, are the roads to adventure in Alaska's interior region.

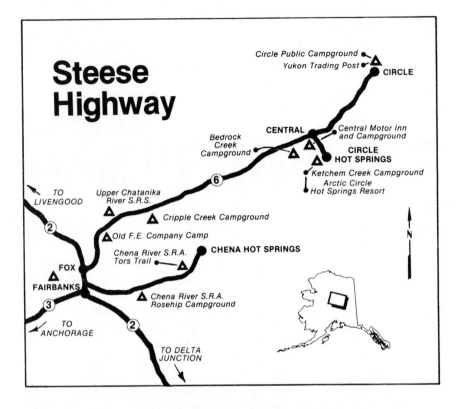

The Steese Highway (Alaska Highway 6)

The Steese Highway begins in Fairbanks at a junction with Airport Way and the Alaska-Richardson Highway and heads northerly on a section of highway called the Steese Expressway. Although most motoring visitors somehow seem to miss the Steese, they should not. It is one of Alaska's most interesting rural highways.

The road is paved for the first 44 miles of its 162 miles. From the end of pavement to the community of Central at Mile 128, the Steese is wide, gravel, and easily traveled. The last 35 miles to the old gold rush city of Circle are narrower, but still negotiable.

Features along the rolling, lightly forested way include two hot springs resorts, recreation areas and trails, fascinating old and new mining operations, and Eagle Summit at Mile 108. During the June 21 summer solstice, the longest day of the year, Fairbanksans and visitors drive up to the summit to enjoy a view of the midnight sun dipping low in the horizon ... *but never quite setting.* Even though the area is located south of the Arctic Circle, and therefore should have at least a brief period of darkness, the 3,624-foot elevation of the summit allows the visitor to keep the sun continuously in view.

Following are campgrounds on the Steese Highway and its side roads.

CHENA RIVER STATE RECREATION AREA (Alaska State Parks)
Access is via Chena Hot Springs Road, which junctions with the Steese at Mile 4.6; campgrounds are located at Mile 27 and Mile 39 Chena Hot Springs Road.

Popular Chena Hot Springs is at the end of the paved 56-mile roadway. Two public campgrounds, both within the .25-million-acre Chena River SRA, are located along the way. (A public picnic area with drinking water and handicap-access toilets is also located at Mile 43, but there are no camping sites there.)

Rosehip Campground at Mile 27 has 38 camping units, 15 picnic units, drinking water, handicap-access toilet facilities, hiking trails, canoe access, and fishing. This is a good choice for motorhomes and trailer rigs. Some campers like to drive out and camp on the river sandbars, which are relatively bug free. **Tors Trail** at Mile 39 has 18 camping units, picnic facilities, drinking water, handicap-access toilets, and hiking/canoeing/fishing opportunities. Camping limit for both campgrounds is 15 days.

Within this very worthwhile recreation area visitors may fish for grayling, watch for wildlife, canoe, kayak, or simply lie in the sunshine beside the crystal-clear waters of the river. Developed hiking trails range from an hour's trek to Angel Rocks to a 3-day trip around the edges of Angel Creek to Chena Dome. A shooting range is also available.

OLD F. E. COMPANY CAMP (private)
Mile 27.9 Steese Highway

UPPER CHATANIKA RIVER STATE RECREATION SITE (Alaska State Parks)
Mile 39 Steese Highway

Here is a pleasant, timbered wayside containing 25 camping units in a 73-acre recreation area. If you prefer informal camping you can drive your RV out on a gravel bar and spend the night there.

A freshwater pump is located near the entrance and the grounds feature picnic facilities, toilets, boat launch, canoe access, and fishing opportunities for grayling. As is frequently the case in the Interior, bugs can be a problem here, so bring along your favorite repellent. (The Upper Chatanika River SRS should not be confused with the Lower Chatanika River SRS, which is located on the Elliott Highway.) Camping limit is 15 days.

This is a popular launching spot for the Chatanika River Canoe Trail, which terminates along the Elliott Highway, also north of Fairbanks. It is a Class II (medium difficulty) river. A popular plan is to access the canoe trail here and haul out at Milepost 11 on the Elliott Highway.

The Chatanika area is rich in gold rush history. Although gold dredges no longer operate in the area, the country is covered with rock and gravel tailings left behind by the dredges during decades of activity.

The dredging process mined millions of dollars' worth of gold-bearing ores, but often the dredges did not succeed in claiming many of the free-flowing gold nuggets that lay in the ground. As a result, many of these unclaimed nuggets remain today, mixed in with the tailings. When, for one reason or another, a contractor has to remove any appreciable amount of such tailings, the place is swarmed over by hordes of hopeful amateur prospectors searching the newly exposed strata.

CRIPPLE CREEK CAMPGROUND (BLM)
Mile 60 Steese Highway

This facility offers 10 sites for tenters as well as 11 for RV travelers. Water is available from pumps and there are toilets, tables, even a nature trail. Unless the water is low, the creek here offers the northernmost access to the Chatanika River Canoe Trail. Camping limit is 7 days.

BEDROCK CREEK CAMPGROUND (Alaska State Parks)
Mile 119 Steese Highway

A small facility, this campground offers 8 sites for campers. There are also picnic tables, toilets, and fishing for grayling. Mosquitoes can be thick so bring repellent and even head nets if you have them. Camping limit is 7 days.

CENTRAL MOTOR INN AND CAMPGROUND (private)
Mile 127.5 Steese Highway

At Mile 128 you come to the small community of Central, where the Circle Hot Springs Road leads 8 miles southerly to historic Arctic Circle Hot Springs Resort.

KETCHEM CREEK CAMPGROUND (Alaska State Parks)
Mile 2.6 Circle Hot Springs Road

Located only 2 miles from the hot springs, this small wayside offers 7 units, toilets, and firewood, but no developed water source. Stream water, however, can be boiled and used. Grayling fishing is fair. Camping limit is 7 days.

ARCTIC CIRCLE HOT SPRINGS RESORT (private)
Mile 8 Circle Hot Springs Road

This is a historic spa much favored during the winter months by miners and prospectors in the gold rush days. It now offers camper parking, fully modern hotel accommodations, cabins, mineral baths and pool, swimming, and gold panning.

CIRCLE PUBLIC CAMPGROUND (city of Circle)
Mile 162 Steese Highway

Until recent years Circle, Alaska, had the farthest-north campground you could drive to in North America. (Inuvik in the Northwest Territories has that honor now. See pages 83–86.) Named by early prospectors in the belief that the site was on the Arctic Circle (it is not, by about 50 miles), the town is a quaint and picturesque, mostly Indian community. Camping is on the banks of the storied Yukon River where tables, toilets, and ample parking are provided.

YUKON TRADING POST (private)
Mile 162 Steese Highway

The Elliott Highway (Alaska Highway 2)

Eleven miles north of Fairbanks at a junction with the Steese Highway, the Elliott Highway begins its meandering northwesterly, then south-westerly journey toward Manley Hot Springs. The distance is 152 miles of which 28 miles are paved. The balance is gravel, clearly negotiable but sometimes a bit rough and sometimes sort of a "roller coaster."

Be on the alert for heavy truck traffic; the Dalton Highway haul road to the North Slope takes off at a junction at about Mile 73, and truckers headed that way can be pretty intimidating. Be cautious, too, when the gravel portions are wet. The bugs at these sites are definitely not timid; bring plenty of mosquito repellent. Following are the campgrounds along this road.

LOWER CHATANIKA RIVER STATE RECREATION SITE (Alaska State Parks)
Mile 10.5 and Mile 11 Elliott Highway

Located on a 570-acre site, this facility offers campsites, picnic shelter, picnic tables, handicap-access toilets, and opportunities for good canoeing and fishing. A large man-made pond is accessible by driving south on the gravel road at Mile 10.5 Elliott Highway. The waters here are popular with swimmers, picnickers, and sunbathers. Facilities are being improved through a cooperative project between Alyeska Pipeline Service Company and Alaska State Parks. Camping limit is 15 days.

At Mile 70.8 is a junction with a short road leading to the nearly vacant town of Livengood, a mining community. Last report we heard is that there were no visitor services there except groceries and gasoline.

At Mile 74 you come to the junction of the Elliott and Dalton highways. The 416-mile Dalton Highway, of course, is the haul road to Prudhoe Bay and the North Slope oilfields. Only the first 210 miles of this road are open to the public. (See Dalton Highway, below.)

TOLVANA BRIDGE (State Department of Highways)
Mile 75 Elliott Highway

This is not really a campground, but self-contained RVs overnight here.

MANLEY HOT SPRINGS RESORT (private)
Mile 151.2 Elliott Highway

Facilities at this resort include RV park, dump station, restaurant, bar, rooms, and pool fed by mineral hot springs.

MANLEY HOT SPRINGS (community)
Mile 152 Elliott Highway

This is another settlement and spa very popular with Alaskans, and Fairbanksans in particular. A public campground is maintained near the springs by the Manley Hot Springs Park Association. (The springs are on a hillside on the right just before you enter town.) A boat launch is also nearby for those who want to try angling for 3-foot-long northern pike, plus grayling and sheefish. There is a $2 daily campground fee.

The Dalton Highway

The Dalton is the haul road to the North Slope oil fields, and it was not built nor is it maintained for the touring visitor. This road is gravel, sometimes rough, and offers only the barest facilities even for RV travelers. There are no motels along the 210-mile section over which it is legal to travel without a permit, and there are only a couple of places to get meals, gas up, or repair your vehicle.

The Alaska Department of Transportation advised us that only two locations have been designated for camping along the Dalton: Arctic Circle at Mile 115 and Marian Creek at Mile 179. These are *not* campgrounds. They are simply old materials storage sites from the pipeline construction days. They contain no water wells, no toilet facilities, nor any other improvements.

If you break down or need help you are pretty much on your own.

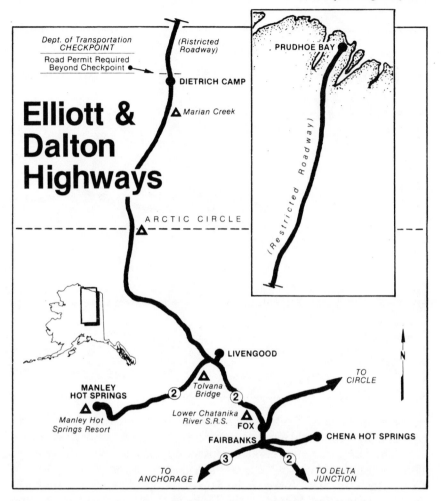

Pipeline supply vehicles probably will not stop to help, although Alaska State Troopers do patrol this road. The speed limit is 45 miles per hour. Hunting is prohibited, as is feeding any wild animals. Carry your own water. It is a good idea to have two spare tires. The mandatory turnaround point for vehicles without permits is at Disaster Creek where the state department of transportation maintains a check station. Only commercial vehicles with permits can continue beyond this point toward Deadhorse and the Arctic Ocean, a distance of some 205 additional miles. Please do not ask for an exception to the turnaround rule: you will not get it.

The Taylor Highway (Alaska Highway 5)

The Taylor Highway leads from Tetlin Junction (at Mile 1301.6 on the Alaska Highway) to Eagle, a distance of some 160 miles over forested rolling

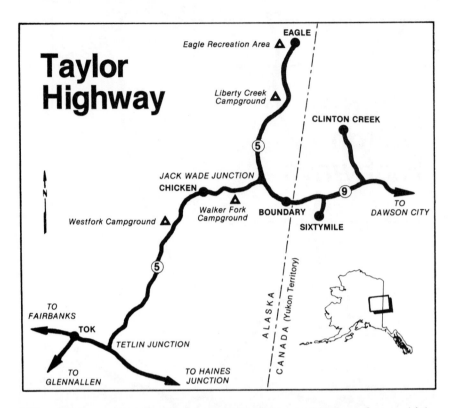

hills and mountains. Traffic is generally light on this road from which, occasionally, derelict old mining equipment can be spotted as well as moose.

There are at least two good reasons for driving the Taylor Highway: to visit the historic old city of Eagle on the Yukon River, and to visit Dawson City in the Canadian Yukon. (The Top of the World Highway begins at Jack Wade Junction, Mile 96 on the Taylor Highway, and leads to Dawson City some 79 miles easterly. Dawson City, in turn, connects via the Klondike Highway with Whitehorse on the Alaska Highway. Taking this loop either coming to or leaving Alaska provides a pleasant alternative to duplicating a large portion of the Alaska Highway, and it offers the opportunity to visit Dawson City on the Yukon River where the Klondike gold rush began. Travelers interested in this option should also see Top of the World Highway, Yukon Highway 9, pages 79–80.)

The Taylor Highway is gravel all the way from Tetlin Junction to Eagle. There are stretches of new construction that are as smooth and wide as you will find anywhere. There are other stretches that are, frankly, pretty rough and narrow; but nothing you can not handle if you keep your speed down. Be especially cautious if there has been much rain.

If you are interested in the road but undecided, we suggest you drive the first dozen miles. They are almost as bad as it gets and if you decide to continue you can be happy in the knowledge that, frequently, the road improves tremendously.

If you are driving to Dawson City, the road on the Canada side is better still. Some of the hill climbs and descents can be a bit steep; caution should be observed by drivers with large motorhomes or trailer rigs. Note, too, that gas can be purchased only at four locations on the Taylor: at Chicken (just off the Taylor Highway at Mile 66.7); at Boundary (nearly ten miles down the road leading to Dawson, east of Jack Wade Junction at Mile 96); at a lodge located at Mile 125.3; and at Eagle.

Here are campgrounds along the Taylor Highway.

WESTFORK CAMPGROUND (BLM)
Mile 48.8 Taylor Highway

A small but scenic campground, the facility has 8 camping spaces, 2 of them pull-throughs, and toilet facilities. The area offers access to the Fortymile National Wild and Scenic River canoe trail. Water from the stream should be boiled or chemically treated before drinking. Picnic tables and fire pits are on-site. This is a perfectly adequate campground but not really exceptional. A much nicer choice, if you are not too tired of driving, is the Walker Fork Campground 33 miles farther up the road. Camping limit is 7 days.

WALKER FORK CAMPGROUND (BLM)
Mile 82 Taylor Highway

This attractive campground is located where Jack Wade Creek and Walker Fork of the Fortymile River meet. The area was dredged in the early days and a very picturesque old dredge hulk is located a few miles up the highway from the campground.

Seventeen ample camper units, many of them pull-throughs, are located in the facility on the left side of the highway northbound; sites for 14 tents are located even more scenically on the right side of the road by the stream.

Other features include picnic tables, fire grates, toilets, and a footbridge to a short hiking trail which leads to the top of limestone bluffs. Drinking water is available from a well on-site. Seven-day limit.

For several miles north from the Walker Fork Campground you drive alongside an active gold-mining operation. It is pretty gruesome. Slow down and make note of it; perhaps it will help take your mind off the worst stretch of washboard along the highway.

At Jade Wade Junction, Mile 95.7 travelers en route to Canada's Yukon should turn east on the gravel road leading to Boundary, the Top of the World Highway, and Dawson City. For a description of camping/driving conditions along this route, see pages 79–80.

LIBERTY CREEK CAMPGROUND (BLM)
Mile 132 Taylor Highway

About 30 miles before you reach Eagle you come to Liberty Creek
Campground with 6 camping units, toilets, picnic tables, and access to
fishing. You can drink the water from the stream, but boil or treat it first.
Historic note: The campground is near the old overnight way station on the
freight-hauling route from Eagle to Chicken. Patriotic miners of the era
called it "the All American Road." Camping limit is 7 days.

EAGLE RECREATION AREA (BLM)
Mile 162 Taylor Highway

This is one of the most scenic campgrounds operated by the BLM in
Alaska. Approximately 15 tent and camper-trailer units are maintained here
on a high bluff overlooking both Mission and American creeks.

Facilities include vault toilets, picnic tables and, usually, natural spring
water. (The spring literally disappears from time to time and a frantic search
ensues to find it at a new location.) This same source at one time provided
water for old Fort Egbert where, in the early 1900s, then-lieutenant Billy
Mitchell served in the United States Army Signal Corps telegraph service.

The BLM has renovated remaining portions of the fort; in the summer
the Eagle Historical Society conducts daily informative free walking tours of
the fort and other areas of historical interest. The town of Eagle is on the
National Register of Historic Places.

A private campground has recently opened in downtown Eagle on the
Yukon River.

The Denali Highway (Alaska Highway 8)

The Denali Highway used to have a well-deserved reputation for being
the roughest, toughest, most car-crumbling road in the North Country. No
longer. The first 21 miles out of Paxson on the Richardson Highway are
paved (though frequently frost-heaved, so keep your speed down), and the
balance of the 114 miles to Cantwell on the George Parks Highway is
negotiable gravel. It can be washboardy when not graded but that is no
problem if you drive slowly.

The pass at 4,086-foot Maclaren Summit is Alaska's second highest
(after 4,800-foot Atigun Pass on the Dalton Highway) but generally presents
no problems.

Over its 135-mile course the road takes in vast tundra meadows,
fantastic views northward of peaks within the Alaska Range, meandering
streams, lakes, and glaciers. More exciting still, the Denali Highway traveler

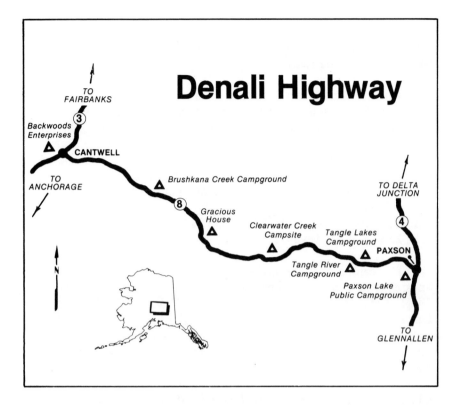

may see wildlife such as caribou, moose, grizzly bears, black bears, Dall mountain sheep, porcupine, foxes, and (more rarely) wolves and wolverines.

At the Cantwell end of the road, the traveler is less than thirty miles from the entrance to Denali National Park and Preserve. In fact, when the Denali Highway opened in 1957 it provided the only driving access to the national park. (The George Parks Highway, with its closer access from Anchorage and Fairbanks, was not finished until the early 1970s.) The Denali is open for traffic only during the late spring, summer, and early fall.

Following are the campgrounds serving travelers along this very scenic route.

PAXSON LAKE PUBLIC CAMPGROUND (BLM)
About 10.5 miles south of Paxson, at Mile 175 on the Richardson (not the Denali) Highway; a 1.5-mile gravel road leads to a camping area near the lake.

Some of the campsites lcoated at his 20-unit campground are on a slope. They could be awkward for RVs. There is a canoe launch at the campground as well as a boat launch accessed over a 200-foot boardwalk. Facilities include a well plus dump station. Fishing for trout and burbot can be productive in the lake. Bring bug repellent. Camping limit is 7 days.

TANGLE LAKES CAMPGROUND (BLM)
Mile 22 Denali Highway

This is the first of two BLM campgrounds whose entrances are located about a fifth of a mile apart. This one is located on the north side of the highway on Round Tangle Lake and contains 14 camping sites, plus toilets, boat launch, stream water (drinkable after boiling or treating), and picnic sites. Berry picking is good in season. The fishing here is for lake trout, grayling, whitefish, and burbot. The boat launch provides access to the Delta National Wild and Scenic River. Camping limit is 7 days.

TANGLE RIVER CAMPGROUND (BLM)
Mile 22 Denali Highway

This campground, located south of the highway, provides 7 camping units; a picnic area; toilets; fireplaces; and launch access to the Tangle River, Tangle Lakes, and the upper Tangle Lakes Canoe Trail, also part of the Delta National Wild and Scenic River. As this book is being written, the water well at the campground is broken. A BLM spokesman indicates it may not be repaired. Camping limit is 7 days. (Some older maps or guidebooks may list this facility as Denali Campground.)

CLEARWATER CREEK CAMPSITE (BLM)
Mile 55.9 Denali Highway

Camping is allowed at this site near the Clearwater Creek bridge. Toilets and litter barrels are located here.

GRACIOUS HOUSE (private)
Mile 82 Denali Highway

BRUSHKANA CREEK CAMPGROUND (BLM)
Mile 105 Denali Highway

Sixteen camping units are located at this streamside campground, which includes toilets, litter barrels, well water, tables, and fire pits. It is situated a short distance from the highway in a timbered setting. Travelers may see moose, bears (both grizzly and black . . . keep your distance), foxes, and caribou in the vicinity. The site is about 60 miles from Denali National Park and Preserve (formerly Mount McKinley National Park).

BACKWOODS ENTERPRISES (private)
Mile 133.9 Denali Highway (about .20 mile beyond the junction with the George Parks Highway).

6

Southcentral
Alaska Highways

T he tiredest joke you hear around this part of the state is that "the best thing about Anchorage is, it is real close to Alaska." Actually, Anchorage is every bit as Alaskan as Nome or Kotzebue or Adak or Aniak. But it is a different kind of Alaska. Anchorage is urban, where nearly half of Alaska's people live. The greatest thing about Anchorage, though, is that within minutes of downtown you can be in country as outrageously wild, or as blessedly comfortable, as your heart desires.

Wild as in running whitewater rapids, skiing glaciers in late evening under summer's midnight sun, scaling mountain peaks, or hiking through bear/moose/wolf-inhabited forests. *Comfortable* as in parking your RV in safe, developed campgrounds; cruising along wide paved highways; and the availability of frequent food and service facilities along the way.

Lots of places, lots of things to see and do here. North of town, via the George Parks or Glenn highways (see Chapter 5), there is the Matanuska Valley with Big Lake and the Nancy Lake State Recreation Area. Farther down the road you come to Denali State Park and Alaska's favorite gathering place for visitors, Denali National Park and Preserve. East and southerly lies Valdez on the Richardson Highway, with spectacular Keystone Canyon; Worthington Glacier; and truly awesome views of the peaks in the Wrangell, Saint Elias, and Chugach mountain ranges.

It is south of Anchorage, however, in the Chugach State Park, the Chugach National Forest, and on the Kenai Peninsula, that southcentral Alaskans most abundantly play, fish, camp, and recreate.

It is not hard to figure out why. There are public-use forest service cabins in the wilderness there for the wonderfully absurd price of only fifteen dollars per night per party. (Write United States Forest Service, 201 East Ninth Avenue, Suite 206, Anchorage, Alaska 99501 for details.) Lunker king salmon in the rivers of the Kenai strain the scales at eighty pounds or more. Hiking trails, some that connect overnight cabins, range from saltwater beaches to alpine heights. Glaciers, like the one at Portage eighty miles south of Anchorage, disgorge icebergs the size of small office buildings. It is fantastic country for the do-it-yourself, see-it-yourself traveler.

The Seward Highway
(Alaska Highways 1 and 9)

The Seward Highway begins in Anchorage and meanders southerly for 127 miles to the city for which it was named. En route the highway skirts Turnagain Arm. (Captain Cook, of eighteenth century exploration fame, came cruising this arm in search of the Northwest Passage to the Atlantic but, unfortunately, he had to "turn again" when he found himself running out of ocean.) The highway parallels the Alaska Railroad as far as the community of Portage, cuts through snowcapped mountains of the Chugach Mountains and ends at Seward on Resurrection Bay in a maritime region of lush greenery. Homesick southeastern Alaskans, sojourning in Southcentral and yearning for salt air and towering spruce, have been known to find complete rejuvenation along the rocky shores of historic Resurrection Bay.

A word about the state highway numbering systems on the Kenai Peninsula, and the mileposts along the roads there: The Seward is highway 1 from Anchorage to Tern Lake Junction, ninety miles from Anchorage; from the junction to Seward it becomes highway 9. The mileposts along both segments of the road measure mileage from Seward to Anchorage, so when you drive from Anchorage south you will start at Mile 127 and end up at Mile 0 when you arrive in Seward. (The Sterling Highway, see pages 148–161, begins at Tern Lake Junction and is designated a continuation of highway 1 until it terminates at Homer on Kachemak Bay. The mileposts on this road, too, show mileage distances from Seward.)

Following are campgrounds along the Seward Highway.

McHUGH CREEK STATE PICNIC SITE (Alaska State Parks)
Mile 111 Seward Highway

This facility, 17 miles south of Anchorage and part of Chugach State Park, is not for overnighting. It is for picnicking only. Tables, handicap-access toilets, and other facilities are located here. Caution: If you are pulling a trailer, do not try to enter this wayside any farther than the parking lot right off the highway. The access road is very steep, with a sharp switchback that would be difficult to maneuver with a rig behind you.

Hiking trails radiate out from the area. The facility is popular with Anchorage motorists, and because of its southern exposure it is usually open year-round.

BIRD CREEK CAMPGROUND (Alaska State Parks)
Mile 101.5 Seward Highway

Also part of Chugach State Park, this 25-unit facility is located in a wooded environment along the shores of Turnagain Arm. Handicap-access toilets and drinking water are on-site. There is even an Anchorage-originating bike trail right through the campground.

Across Turnagain Arm is a view of the Chugach Mountains and the old gold-mining community of Hope. Fishing can be productive for pink salmon and Dolly Varden. Caution: Do not venture out on the mud flats of Turnagain Arm. You could easily get stuck there, with tragic results.

BJ GAS, GROCERY AND CAMPER PARK (private)
Mile 100.8 Seward Highway

SCOTTISH INN (private)
Mile 100.7 Seward Highway

At Mile 90, the Seward Highway junctions with the road leading to Girdwood, historic Crow Creek Mine, and Alyeska Resort. A private campground is located at Crow Creek Mine and free camping is permitted (though there are no developed facilities) at Alyeska Resort, the state's largest and best-known private winter and summer recreation center.

BEAVER POND CAMPGROUND (USFS)
BLACK BEAR CAMPGROUND (USFS)
WILLIWAW CAMPGROUND (USFS)
All three accessed by the Portage Glacier access road which junctions with the Seward Highway at Mile 79.

Although they are designated as three different campgrounds, these areas are located within a mile of each other at Mile 2.9, Mile 3.7, and Mile 4.1 on the Portage Glacier access road which junctions with the Seward Highway 48 miles southeast of Anchorage. The access road ends 1.3 miles beyond Williwaw at Mile 5.4 where the USFS has constructed the Begich-Boggs Visitor Center on the shores of Portage Lake. A large paved parking area provides views of Portage Glacier and lake. A unique experience awaits the traveler who stops there; the opportunity to actually *touch* an iceberg which has been pulleyed into the structure.

A lodge is located here as well, in case you want to take a break from camping or camp cooking. The campgrounds are all located on the right side of the road as you drive toward the center. Portage Valley offers a fascinating

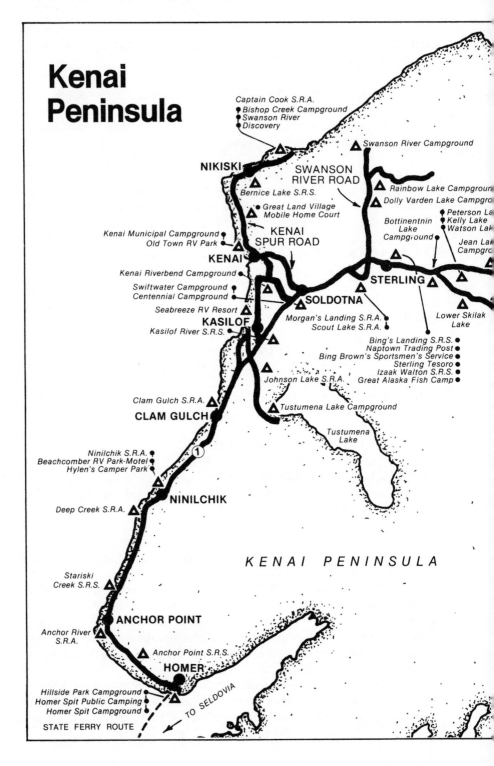

Kenai Peninsula

Captain Cook S.R.A.
Bishop Creek Campground
Swanson River
Discovery

Swanson River Campground

NIKISKI

SWANSON RIVER ROAD

Bernice Lake S.R.S.

Rainbow Lake Campground
Dolly Varden Lake Campground

Great Land Village
Mobile Home Court

Bottinentnin Lake Campground

Peterson Lake
Kelly Lake
Watson Lake

KENAI SPUR ROAD

Jean Lake Campground

Kenai Municipal Campground
Old Town RV Park

KENAI

Kenai Riverbend Campground

STERLING

Swiftwater Campground
Centennial Campground

Seabreeze RV Resort

SOLDOTNA

Lower Skilak Lake

KASILOF

Kasilof River S.R.S.

Morgan's Landing S.R.A.
Scout Lake S.R.A.

Bing's Landing S.R.S.
Naptown Trading Post
Bing Brown's Sportsmen's Service
Sterling Tesoro
Izaak Walton S.R.S.
Great Alaska Fish Camp

Johnson Lake S.R.A.

Clam Gulch S.R.A.

Tustumena Lake Campground

CLAM GULCH

Tustumena Lake

Ninilchik S.R.A.
Beachcomber RV Park-Motel
Hylen's Camper Park

NINILCHIK

Deep Creek S.R.A.

K E N A I   P E N I N S U L A

Stariski Creek S.R.S.

ANCHOR POINT

Anchor River S.R.A.

Anchor Point S.R.S.

HOMER

Hillside Park Campground
Homer Spit Public Camping
Homer Spit Campground

TO SELDOVIA

STATE FERRY ROUTE

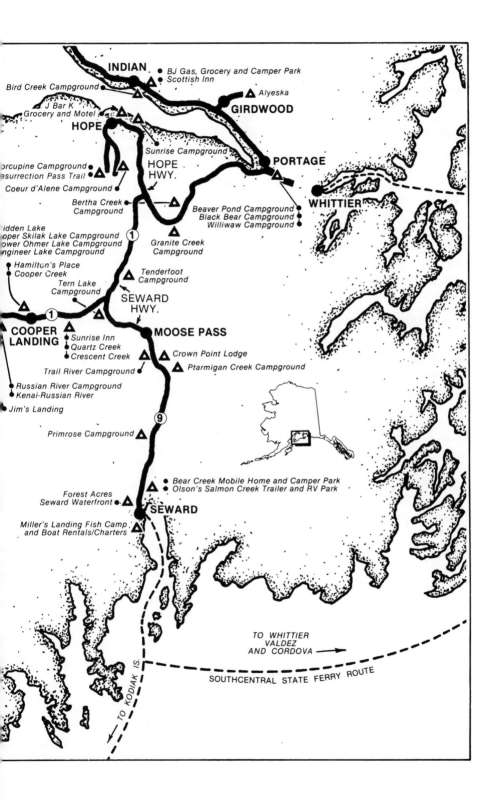

study in the ways of nature. Snow avalanches (in winter only, fortunately) sometimes wipe out trees and vegetation even on the valley floor.

The winds here can be fearsome even in summer. If you see foul-weather warning signs placed on Portage Glacier access road it would be best to postpone your visit. Winds can blow as hard as 100 miles an hour. In the past, hurricane-force velocities have literally peeled back the edges of the blacktop paving on the parking lot!

Vegetation in the area is primarily willow and white spruce. From many of the campsites, hanging glaciers are observable high in the surrounding mountains. Moose may sometimes be seen here as well as black bears and mountain goats. **Beaver Pond Campground** has 7 camping and 3 picnic units; **Blackbear** has 12 camping units; and **Williwaw** has 36 camping and 6 picnic spaces.

You may also hike the 1-mile Byron Glacier trail, which leaves from the parking area, for a closer view of Byron Glacier. Turn off at Mile 5.2 to reach the parking area.

Camping limit at these sites is 14 days; $5 daily fee.

BERTHA CREEK CAMPGROUND (USFS)
Mile 65.6 Seward Highway

Twelve camping units are located in this campground situated in cottonwood trees by the water. A short trail leads uphill to a commanding view. Looking landward you see typical Interior trees and environment; seaward you gaze upon typical coastal forest conditions.

Moose and Dall sheep are sometimes sighted in this locale. This is former placer mining country, and traces of mining activity can be found by scouting around the area. Toilets, fireplaces, and drinking water are on-site. Camping limit is 14 days; $5 daily fee.

GRANITE CREEK CAMPGROUND (USFS)
Mile 63 Seward Highway

Although this campground is called Granite Creek, this is actually the meeting place of Granite Creek, Bench Creek, and Center Creek where they form the East Fork of Sixmile Creek.

There are three groups of camping units here. As you enter and drive the circular loop, keep to the right, and we recommend you bypass the first units you come to. They are adequate but are set among thick scrub timber, not nearly so satisfying as the setting near the creek itself.

Best yet is the group of units located beyond the creek and water pump. This latter group sits among more open stands of spruce with thick moss carpet. Old-timers in the area say there is a good duck pond in the high country at the head of nearby Lynx Creek. Moose can be seen in the valleys.

A total of 20 camping units are located here, plus toilets, fireplaces, and drinking water. Fishing can be productive for Dolly Varden. Fee is $5; camping limit is 14 days.

SUNRISE CAMPGROUND (private)
Accessed from the Hope Highway.

J BAR K GROCERY AND MOTEL (private)
Accessed from the Hope Highway.

COEUR d'ALENE CAMPGROUND (USFS)
RESURRECTION PASS TRAIL (USFS)

PORCUPINE CAMPGROUND (USFS)
Accessed from the Hope Highway, which junctions with and heads northwest from the Seward Highway at Mile 56.7.

There are two good reasons for utilizing these campgrounds, in addition to the pleasures of the sites themselves: the town of Hope, and a fabulous 38-mile hiking trail.

The town of Hope is located near the end of the paved 17-mile Hope Highway. The community, founded in 1888, was once a bustling gold rush center. Now it is nearly a ghost town; only a handful of real old-timers remain. But Hope is having a revival of sorts, particularly among Anchorage folk who want a place to get away from it all. Motel, grocery, gas, and other visitor facilities are available.

Close to the town, two side roads fork out from the main Hope Road. The Palmer Creek road, which is steep and rather narrow, leads to the left through birch groves to a high, pleasant campground called **Coeur d'Alene**. Six camping units are located here, about 7.5 miles south of Hope. This probably is not a good choice for big rigs or trailers. The fishing is for pink salmon and Dolly Varden. Camping limit is 14 days. Toilet facilities are provided but there is no developed water source. There is no fee for camping. Up the road about 2 miles lies the old Hershey mine, which you might wish to visit.

The right fork from the Hope Road leads up Resurrection Creek past homesteads and mines to the beginning of the 38-mile **USFS Resurrection Pass Trail**. This is an outstanding route, on which 8 USFS public-use cabins are located, each less than a day's hike apart. The trail terminates at Mile 52.3 near Cooper Landing on the Sterling Highway. Cabin permits are issued at Chugach National Forest offices and must be carried with you in order to use a shelter. Because the trail is so popular, cabin stays are limited to 3 days, May 15 through August 31, and for 7 days the rest of the year.

At the end of the Hope Road is **Porcupine Campground**, with 24 camping units, toilets, drinking water, and fishing for pinks and Dollies. Camping limit here is 14 days; there is a $5 daily fee.

TENDERFOOT CAMPGROUND (USFS)
Mile 46 Seward Highway

The side road leading to this campground turns left (if you are traveling south) off the Seward Highway at Summit Lake. The road leads around the end of the lake to the east side. Twenty-seven camping units are set among attractive stands of white spruce. Although there are lush carpets of moss on the ground, a sparseness of underbrush gives one the feeling of openness. The lake, which offers canoeing and good Dolly Varden fishing, is visible through the trees from most sites. Drinking water is available, as are handicap-access toilet facilities, boat landing, tables, and fireplaces. Daily fee is $5; camping limit is 14 days.

TERN LAKE CAMPGROUND (USFS)
Mile 37.3 Seward Highway

At Tern Lake Junction the Seward and Sterling highways meet. The Seward (which now becomes Alaska Highway 9) continues southeasterly to Moose Pass and Seward; the Sterling Highway (which is now designated Alaska Highway 1, see pages 148–161) heads southwesterly to Cooper Landing and eventually Homer. Tern Lake campground has 25 camping units, which are placed among stands of birch and spruce. Some of the sites overlook the lake. This lake derives its name from the arctic tern, a bird that makes its summer home here. Watch out if you get too close to their nests. They will dive at you to protect their territory. On-site are toilets, drinking water, canoe launch, fishing for Dolly Varden. Daily fee is $5; camping limit is 14 days.

TRAIL RIVER CAMPGROUND (USFS)
Mile 24.1 Seward Highway

This is one of Alaska's larger campgrounds, with 86 camping units, picnic tables and fireplaces, toilets, even a volleyball and horseshoe area. The camping sites are located on a number of loops within the grounds. Depending on the loop you select, you may enjoy a spruce forest setting where berries carpet the ground; a location among glistening birch trees; or the camping site of many a visitor's dream alongside the waters of Kenai Lake. Because of its size the campground tends to be a bit complex. If you drive off from your camp make special note of its location, otherwise you could have a hard time finding it again. There is good fishing for Dolly Varden, rainbow trout, and lake trout in the river. Camping limit is 14 days; $5 daily fee.

CROWN POINT LODGE (private)
Mile 24 Seward Highway

PTARMIGAN CREEK CAMPGROUND (USFS)
Mile 23.1 Seward Highway

The USFS has located 20 camping units at this campground, situated in rather dark and heavy spruce stands alongside Ptarmigan Creek. A nearby trail leads to Ptarmigan Lake where the fishing is good for rainbows and Dollies. In season there is also good mountain goat hunting in the area. Facilities include toilets and drinking water. Camping limit is 14 days; $5 daily fee.

PRIMROSE CAMPGROUND (USFS)
Mile 17.2 Seward Highway

This campground, also called Primrose Landing, is much enjoyed by boaters. Located at the lower end of Kenai Lake (accessed by a 1-mile-long road from the highway), the campground contains 10 camping units, drinking water, a surfaced boat ramp, and a large parking lot for vehicles and boat trailers.

Evidence of the 1964 earthquake can still be seen in this area where the heaving earth literally split trees in two and the land sank, drowning trees on the edge of the lake.

Three developed picnic spots are pleasantly inaccessible except by boat: Meadow Creek Picnic Area, Ship Creek Picnic Area, and Porcupine Island Picnic Area. Camping limit is 14 days; $5 daily fee.

BEAR CREEK MOBILE HOME and CAMPER PARK (private)
Mile 6.6 Seward Highway

OLSON'S SALMON CREEK TRAILER AND RV PARK (private)
Mile 3.2 Seward Highway

FOREST ACRES (city of Seward)
Mile 2.5 Seward Highway

Forest Acres is a municipal campground located on the right side of the highway as you drive to Seward. Facilities include flush toilets and drinking water. There is a $4 daily fee; 14-day camping limit.

SEWARD WATERFRONT (city of Seward)
Located downtown on the shores of Resurrection Bay.

This is one of southcentral Alaska's favorite overnighting places. RV camping is allowed at designated parking spaces. Facilities include a surfaced boat ramp, flush toilets, city drinking water, dump station, plus restaurants, snack bars, small-boat fishing charters, and other visitor services. Daily fee is $4; camping limit is 14 days.

MILLER'S LANDING FISH CAMP and BOAT RENTALS/ CHARTERS (private)
Located at Lowell Point on Resurrection Bay 2 miles south of Seward.

The Sterling Highway
(Continuation of Alaska Highway 1)

The Seward and Sterling highways meet at Tern Lake Junction. The Seward (which now becomes Alaska Highway 9) continues southeasterly to Moose Pass and Seward; the Sterling Highway (which is now designated Alaska Highway 1) heads southwesterly to Cooper Landing and eventually Homer. The mileposts along the road measure distance from Seward.

The Sterling Highway is a modern, paved 136-mile roadway to Homer and the maritime joys of Kachemak Bay. The highway is, itself, a pleasurable visitor experience, sometimes going through the two-million-acre, moose-filled Kenai National Wildlife Refuge and at other times skirting the salmon-rich shores of Cook Inlet. This is also first-class freshwater fishing country and the highway provides easy access to productive streams and lakes.

Of particular interest to the canoe enthusiast are the renowned Swan Lake, Swanson River, and Kenai River canoe trails in the Kenai National Wildlife Refuge, under the jurisdiction of the United States Fish and Wildlife Service. Small wonder that this road can be one of Alaska's most crowded on holidays and weekends, which makes it a logical choice for weekday travel if you have that option. Here are the campgrounds, starting with Tern Lake (also listed in the Seward Highway section), along the Sterling Highway.

TERN LAKE CAMPGROUND (USFS)
Mile 37.3 Seward Highway; also the beginning of the Sterling Highway.

The Tern Lake campground has 25 camping units, which are placed among stands of birch and spruce. Some of the sites overlook the lake. The lake derives its name from the arctic tern, a bird that makes its summer home here. Watch out if you get too close to their nests. They will dive at you to protect their territory. On-site are toilets, drinking water, canoe launch, and fishing for Dolly Varden. Daily fee is $5; 14-day limit.

SUNRISE INN (private)
Mile 45 Sterling Highway

QUARTZ CREEK CAMPGROUND (USFS)
CRESCENT CREEK CAMPGROUND (USFS)
Both USFS campgrounds at Mile 45 Sterling Highway.

Quaking aspen gives a pleasant sunny feeling to **Quartz Creek Campground** on Quartz Creek road about 1/3 mile off the Sterling Highway. A small-boat ramp gives access to deep water and there is a good sandy swimming beach. A trail (sometimes muddy) leads along Quartz Creek for anglers seeking rainbows or Dolly Varden. This campground contains 26 camping units and flush toilets, a rarity in Alaska public campgrounds. There is also a dump station.

Dall Sheep can sometimes be spotted on the mountainsides. Canoeing is popular between this campground and Crescent Creek Campground, which is located 3 miles down the road. Daily fee is $6 instead of the usual USFS $5 fee; camping limit is 14 days.

Crescent Creek Campground, at the confluence of Quartz and Crescent creeks some 3 miles down Quartz Creek road from the Sterling Highway, contains 9 camping units set among quaking aspen, birch, and occasional spruce. Moose can sometimes be seen at the end of clearings.

Although Quartz Creek is not actually designated a canoe trail, it is possible to canoe from this campground down the creek to Kenai Lake. Some fallen trees may block the stream in places. The fishing here is for grayling. The site contains water and toilet facilities. Daily fee is $5; camping limit is 14 days.

HAMILTON'S PLACE (private)
Mile 48.5 Sterling Highway

COOPER CREEK CAMPGROUND (USFS)
Mile 50.5 Sterling Highway

This campground seems like two, since sites have been located on both sides of the Sterling Highway. The sites along the Kenai River offer the view (and marvelous sounds) of rushing water. There is enough beach alongside the stream for a family game of baseball, provided it has not rained a lot.

Sites on the other side of the road are set among spruce trees on the shores of Cooper Creek. It is possible you might see moose feeding in the still ponds of the area. Fishing is for Dolly Varden; rainbow trout; silver, pink, and red salmon. Twenty-four camping units are located here, along with tables, fireplaces, toilets, and water. Camping limit is 14 days; daily fee is $5.

RUSSIAN RIVER CAMPGROUND (USFS)
Mile 52.8 Sterling Highway

There are two Russian River camping facilities. One campground is operated by the USFS, and down the road at Mile 55 is the Kenai-Russian River Campground under the jurisdiction of the USFWS. The USFS site contains 84 camping units, drinking water, and flush toilets.

If you are heading westerly toward Homer you reach the campground by turning left onto a 1-mile-long access road. The Russian River offers some of the best river salmon fishing in Alaska, as well as angling for rainbows and Dollies. A hikers-only trail leads from here to Russian Lakes where you will find excellent trout angling.

Gold was discovered on this river by a Russian-American Company prospector in 1848; the same year the big California rush began, and 50 years before the Klondike stampede. The Russians, however, had no interest in gold. They were too busy exploiting the country's fur resources, and suppressed news of the gold strike.

The campground has tables and fireplaces, a fish-cleaning station, and a dump station. Bears sometimes frequent the premises. Fees here are slightly higher than at other USFS campgrounds. A single occupancy RV will cost $6 daily; double occupancy is $8 daily. The camping limit is 3 days during peak fishing periods, at other times it is 14 days. In spite of its large size, this site fills up early, especially on weekends and holidays.

KENAI-RUSSIAN RIVER (USFWS)
Mile 55 Sterling Highway

Like the USFS campground just up the road a bit, this wayside is extremely popular during the fishing season and fills up early, especially on weekends and holidays. Fishing here is for rainbow trout; Dolly Varden; silver, pink, and red salmon. The best fishing, incidentally, is on the river shore opposite the campgrounds. A small commercial ferry carries anglers across the water for $3.

The USFWS has located 180 camping units here, along with toilets, tables in many units, and a developed drinking water system. Camping limit is 3 days. The daily fee schedule is: parking for 30 minutes or less, free; parking for up to 3 hours, $4; overnight stay using 1 space, $6, and using 2 spaces, $8. Collecting the fees has been contracted by the USFWS to Sportsman's Lodge, of Cooper Landing.

At Mile 58, the Sterling Highway junctions with nineteen-mile Skilak Lake Road, a loop which was formerly part of the Sterling Highway and which rejoins the main highway at Mile 75.2 Sterling Highway. Along the loop are a series of campgrounds bounded by woods and waters and developed by the USFWS. The USFWS maintains an information center at the Mile 58 junction. There, visitors can obtain the latest data on fishing hot spots, wildlife viewing areas, and points of scenic interest.

JIM'S LANDING (USFWS)
Mile .5 Skilak Lake Road

This is a small (5 units), often-crowded camping area with drinking water, toilet facilities, boat landing, and canoeing opportunities on the Kenai River. Angling is for rainbow trout; Dolly Varden; silver, red, and pink salmon. There is no fee; camping limit is 14 days.

HIDDEN LAKE (USFWS)
Mile 5 Skilak Lake Road

Another popular and often crowded campground, Hidden Lake wayside offers 30 camping spaces, toilets, drinking water, boat landing, and canoeing. Water ski buffs, as well as fishermen, utilize this lake. Fish here include rainbow trout, lake trout, Dolly Varden, and kokanee (landlocked red salmon). No fee; 7-day camping limit.

UPPER SKILAK LAKE CAMPGROUND (USFWS)
Mile 8.6 Skilak Lake Road

Skilak Lake, at 24,000 surface acres, is one of the largest lakes on the Kenai Peninsula. It is also one of the most dangerous for boaters when storm winds come up. Caution: Boaters are advised to stay near shore and to always wear life jackets as storm winds can come up fast and without warning. The campground itself has 10 units, toilets, drinking water, fire grates, and a boat ramp. A nearby offshore rock island provides an interesting nesting site for a large colony of gulls.

Fish caught in these waters include rainbows, lake trout, Dolly Varden, silver and red salmon, and whitefish. No fee; 14-day camping limit.

LOWER OHMER LAKE CAMPGROUND (USFWS)
Mile 8.8 Skilak Lake Road

A very small campground (4 units), it is nonetheless one of the peninsula's most scenic, surrounded by rolling forested hills with the Kenai Mountains in the distance. For the fisherman, this is a really great rainbow lake, either from shore or boat. A boat landing is located here. There are toilets but no drinking water wells. No fee; 14-day camping limit.

ENGINEER LAKE CAMPGROUND (USFWS)
Mile 9.5 Skilak Lake Road

Silver salmon is the fish of choice for anglers in this lake. Eight camping units are located here but no toilets and no developed drinking water source. Nonetheless, it is a popular camping spot, and because of its southern exposure, it is usually open year-round. There is a boat landing site. A fairly level 7-mile trail takes off from the parking lot here and connects Engineer Lake with Hidden, Kelly, Peterson, and other smaller bodies of water. No fee; 14-day camping limit.

LOWER SKILAK LAKE (USFWS)
Mile 15 Skilak Lake Road

As we mentioned previously at the Upper Skilak Campground listing, this can be a very productive fishing lake; but it can also be very dangerous when sudden storm winds arise. Do not venture out in a small boat, in any craft stay within easy return distance to shore, and always wear life jackets.

Fish in these waters include rainbow trout, lake trout, Dolly Varden, silver and red salmon, and whitefish. It is possible to hike the shore to the right in order to fish the lake's outlet. Nature note: Bears have been known to visit this campground, and red squirrels are particularly active in this area in the fall. You can watch them tossing cones from high tree limbs to the ground, then scrambling down to cache them among tree roots for the winter. Fourteen camping units are located here, with toilets, drinking water, fire grates, and boat launch. No fee; 14-day limit.

BOTTINENTNIN LAKE CAMPGROUND (USFWS)
Mile 19 Skilak Lake Road

A very small campground (3 units) on an extremely shallow lake (8 feet to 10 feet deep). There are no toilets and no developed water source. Bottinentnin is quite popular with boaters and, in the fall, berry pickers. Red salmon have been stocked here.

JEAN LAKE CAMPGROUND (USFWS)
Mile 59.8 Sterling Highway

This wayside is also very small, with 3 camping units, picnic facilities, toilets, drinking water, and boat launch. Rainbows and Dollies are the species to fish for. No fee; 14-day camping limit.

PETERSON LAKE CAMPGROUND (USFWS)
KELLY LAKE CAMPGROUND (USFWS)
Access road to both waysides at Mile 68.5 Sterling Highway.

Boat ramps are available at both of these 3-unit sites, as are toilets, water, tables, and fire grates. Visitors at both sites may well see the giant Kenai moose for which the peninsula is famous. Access is available to the Seven Lakes Trail. Peterson and Kelly lakes are particularly good rainbow trout waters for the fly fisherman. No fee; 14-day limit.

WATSON LAKE CAMPGROUND (USFWS)
Mile 70.8 Sterling Highway

Another 3-unit facility, equipped with toilets, fire grates, and boat launch, but no developed drinking water source. Fly-fishing for rainbows is good here, and there reportedly is good red salmon angling in season. Watson is frequently used as a base for moose hunters after the season opens in mid-August.

BING'S LANDING STATE RECREATION SITE (Alaska State Parks)
Mile 80.2 Sterling Highway

This is not only a camping area (24 spaces, handicap-access toilets, and water), it is also a major boat-launching spot for upriver boating above the nearby and turbulent Naptown Rapids. The rapids are rated Class III (difficult) and provide a credible challenge if you are into the rapids-running mania.

Local (and possibly "loco") divers in wet suits, buoyancy vests, flippers, and masks have also taken to running these rapids; an activity only the very skilled should attempt. No fee; camping limit is 7 days June through August, 15 days the rest of the year.

NAPTOWN TRADING POST (private)
Mile 80.9 Sterling Highway

BING BROWN'S SPORTSMEN'S SERVICE (private)
Mile 81 Sterling Highway

STERLING TESORO (private)
Mile 81.7 Sterling Highway

IZAAK WALTON STATE RECREATION SITE (Alaska State Parks)
Mile 82 Sterling Highway

This recently rehabilitated facility where the Kenai River meets the Moose River offers 38 camping units, picnic sites, handicap-access toilets, fresh water, and boat launch to the Kenai River. Also available in the area are canoe rentals and shuttle service to the much-acclaimed Swan Lake and Swanson River canoe trails.

Angling in the campground area is for rainbow trout; Dolly Varden; silver, king, red, and pink salmon. During peak times, several hundred visitors will be on-site. No camping fee; camping limit is 7 days June through August, 15 days the rest of the year.

GREAT ALASKA FISH CAMP (private)
Mile 82 Sterling Highway

DOLLY VARDEN LAKE CAMPGROUND (USFWS)
Accessible via the Swanson River Road, which junctions with the Sterling Highway at Mile 83.8.

Located 15 miles up the Swanson River Road, Dolly Varden Lake Campground has 12 camping units, toilets, drinking water, fire grates, and boat launch site. A big RV or trailer might have some difficulty, especially turning around, in this area. In spite of its name, the principal fishing here is for rainbow trout and arctic char. No fee; 14-day limit for campers.

RAINBOW LAKE CAMPGROUND (USFWS)
Accessible via the Swanson River Road, which junctions with the Sterling Highway at Mile 83.8.

Located 1 mile beyond Dolly Varden Lake, Rainbow Lake Campground is small (4 units), has toilets, water, fire grates, and a boat launch area. Fishing is good for rainbows.

SWANSON RIVER CAMPGROUND (USFWS)
Accessible via the Swanson River Road, which junctions with the Sterling Highway at Mile 83.8.

Swanson River Campground is located at Mile 18 on the Swanson River Road and contains 8 camping units, toilets, water, tables, fire grates, and boat launch. Fishing is for rainbow trout, Dolly Varden, and silver salmon. At the river you can launch your canoe and paddle downstream to a take-out point at the Captain Cook SRA (see page 156) 1 or 2 days later.

MORGAN'S LANDING STATE RECREATION AREA (Alaska State Parks)
SCOUT LAKE STATE RECREATION AREA (Alaska State Parks)
Both areas accessible via Scout Lake Loop Road at Mile 85 Sterling Highway.

The Kenai area office of Alaska State Parks is located about 4 miles down the loop road (follow the signs) and can provide you with up-to-the-minute details about fishing and other conditions at these and other campgrounds on the Kenai Peninsula. **Morgan's Landing SRA** is a 300-plus-acre parcel on the north shore of the Kenai River. Easily accessed shore fishing can be quite productive here, depending on the season, for rainbows; Dollies; silver, king, red, and pink salmon. There are no launching facilities: the area is closed to fishing from boats May 15 through July 31. Bald eagles, moose, and a variety of waterfowl are frequent visitors to the area. There are no developed camping units but handicap-access toilets, water, and picnic accommodations are on-site.

Nearby **Scout Lake SRA** contains 8 camping spaces and offers water, handicap-access toilets, and a covered picnic shelter. Fishing is for landlocked king salmon. A pleasant trail leads to the lake and a sandy swimming beach. A couple of miles of hiking and water ski trails adjoin the picnic area.

No fees; there are 15-day camping limits at these facilities.

SWIFTWATER CAMPGROUND (city of Soldotna)
On East Redoubt Road, accessed at Mile 94 Sterling Highway.
CENTENNIAL CAMPGROUND (city of Soldotna)
On Kalifornsky Beach Road, accessed at Mile 96 Sterling Highway.

These campgrounds are in wooded settings on the banks of the Kenai River and both offer boat ramps. Fishing at these sites is for rainbow trout; Dolly Varden; silver, pink, red, and king salmon. Wildlife in the area includes bears, moose, eagles, and loons.

Swiftwater has 20 camping units; Centennial has a whopping 179. There are toilet facilities, developed drinking water sources, and dump stations at each location. These campgrounds can be quite crowded on weekends and holidays; plan to arrive early. Daily fee is $5 at each location; 14-day limits.

At Mile 94.2, the Sterling Highway junctions with the Kenai Spur Road. Following are commercial and public campgrounds on this modern paved road.

KENAI MUNICIPAL CAMPGROUND (city of Kenai)
City is located at Mile 11 Kenai Spur Road; campground is on Forest Drive.

Forty camping units are located here in a lovely wooded setting overlooking Cook Inlet. Playground, shelters, toilet facilities, and drinking water are among its features. There is also fishing for pink, red, king, and silver salmon. Camping limit is 72 hours.

OLD TOWN RV PARK (private)
On Main Street in Kenai.

GREAT LAND VILLAGE MOBILE HOME COURT (private)
Mile 19.1 Kenai Spur Road

BERNICE LAKE STATE RECREATION SITE (Alaska State Parks)
Mile 23 Kenai Spur Road

This recreation site, located on a peninsula that juts into Bernice Lake 10 miles north of Kenai, contains 11 camping units, plus water, handicap-access toilet facilities, boat launching site, small swimming beach, and pleasurable canoeing/kayaking. Only a few years ago this was considered a rather remote wayside. The construction of petrochemical plants in the region has put this site in the very heart of the Kenai industrial area. No fee; 15-day camping limit.

CAPTAIN COOK STATE RECREATION AREA (Alaska State Parks)
Miles 36-39 Kenai Spur Road

Probably because it is at the end of the road, this is one of the relatively undiscovered golden nuggets of Alaska camping. Spread over nearly 3,500 acres, Captain Cook SRA contains 1 site for tents, 1 remote campground, 2 sites for RVs and tents, plus picnic areas and the terminus of the Swanson River canoe trail.

Twelve tent-only camping units are located at Bishop Creek Campground, Mile 36 on the spur road. Ten remote boat-in only camping spaces are provided at Stormy Lake Remote Campground. At Miles 36-37, road-accessible Stormy Lake facilities include 100 parking places, picnic shelters and facilities, dressing rooms, swimming beach, swim float, boat launch, and toilets. One camping unit is at Swanson River, and there are 53 at Discovery Campground.

Discovery deserves special mention. This is a locale of rolling hills, wooded spruce plateaus, and beautiful vistas of the Alaska Range across Cook Inlet. Mount Spurr, Mount Redoubt, and especially Mount Iliamna are prominent across the water (so are 13 oil platforms in the inlet). A trail leads from Discovery to the Swanson River tidelands. Observe the warning signs in the area, and do not let an incoming tide catch you off guard.

Interpretative programs are scheduled regularly during the summer season.

Berries are thick in the area, but avoid the bright red or white poisonous baneberry; and if you get into a berry-picking standoff with a bear, leave the berries to him. Do not even think of trying to bluff or shoo him away.

There is no charge for the use of this campground; there is a 15-day camping limit.

Kalifornsky Beach Road junctions with the Sterling Highway at Mile 96. A very short distance down the road is Centennial Park Campground (see page 155 for description). At Mile 4.7 on Kalifornsky Beach Road the Ciechansky Loop Road and Port Road leads to Kenai Riverbend Campground (private). At Mile 13.3 on Kalifornsky Beach Road is privately operated Seabreeze RV Resort.

KASILOF RIVER STATE RECREATION AREA (Alaska State Parks)
Mile 109.5 Sterling Highway

Sixteen camping units are located here, as are handicap-access toilet facilities, drinking water, picnic tables, and fishing for king salmon. No fee; 15-day camping limit.

JOHNSON LAKE STATE RECREATION AREA (Alaska State Parks)
Mile 110 Sterling Highway

Located on the shores of Johnson Lake with 50 camping spaces, handicap-access toilets, drinking water, boat landing site, and often some first-class rainbow fishing. This hourglass-shaped lake is nearly 1 mile long. The campground is located at the "waist" of the lake. A number of the camping units are pull-throughs. You may see beavers in the waters here as well as moose. You also may see two-legged critters in the water; there is some swimming here. Motorized watercraft are prohibited. No charge; 15-day camping limit.

TUSTUMENA LAKE CAMPGROUND (USFWS)
On 6-mile access road at Mile 110 Sterling Highway.

Although the name would indicate otherwise, this campground is actually located on the Kasilof River about 1 mile downstream from Tustumena Lake. The river is swift but, with care, boats in the 20- to 25-foot class can be launched and make it to the lake. This is a popular campground; it officially has 10 spaces but frequently contains several more users. There is no developed drinking water source but toilet facilities and fire grates are located at the site.

Tustumena is a large body of water and subject to extremely hazardous winds from the nearby Harding Icefield. These winds can arise at a moment's notice and the lake can change from dead calm to deadly, with 5- to 6-foot waves (sometimes even greater). This is absolutely no place for a small skiff with a kicker. Fishing is for lake trout, Dolly Varden, whitefish, and silver salmon. No charge for camping here; there is a 14-day limit.

CLAM GULCH STATE RECREATION AREA (Alaska State Parks)
Mile 117 Sterling Highway

As the name implies, this is superb razor clam digging country. Literally thousands of clams are dug, steamed, and consumed here each year. (Note: You must have a current Alaska fishing license to dig for clams.) There are no designated camping units. A gravel road leads from the Sterling Highway to the large parking/camping area. Handicap-access toilets, water, and picnic tables are on-site. A steep 4-wheel-drive-only road leads to the beach. Be careful near the ocean bluffs; a fall could be fatal. No fee for camping; there is a 15-day camping limit.

NINILCHIK STATE RECREATION AREA (Alaska State Parks)
Miles 134.5, 135.1, and 135.4 Sterling Highway

There are 3 camping areas at this SRA: A new development at Mile 134.5 provides for more than 40 campers near the Ninilchik River; there is parking/camping actually on the beach for about 125 RVs at Mile 135.1; and 9 units at Mile 135.4 overlook the beach. Handicap-access toilets are on-site and drinking water is available in all areas except the beach. There is also a dump station adjacent to the bluff-overlook campground.

Boat ramp facilities are provided at Ninilchik Beach. Fishing is for Dolly Varden; steelhead trout; king, silver, and pink salmon. Ninilchik is actually two separate communities. The new town sits right beside the highway on a high bluff overlooking Cook Inlet. The old village, located at the base of the bluff, had its origins when Russian fur traders colonized the area in 1820. The scenery, with volcanic mountains across the inlet and the onion-domed Russian Orthodox church on a nearby hill, is spectacular. Camping limit is 15 days; no fee.

BEACHCOMBER RV PARK-MOTEL (private)
Mile 135.1 Sterling Highway

HYLEN'S CAMPER PARK (private)
Kingsley Road off Sterling Highway at Mile 135.4.

DEEP CREEK STATE RECREATION AREA (Alaska State Parks)
Mile 138 Sterling Highway

Another much-used recreation area, this one features clamming, saltwater surf fishing, freshwater angling, and the simple joys of beach walking. Like the Ninilchik beach area, spaces here are not developed; you simply park and camp in the designated locale. One year a few years back nearly 28,000 visitors overnighted here. Locals frequently roam the beach with the visitors picking up free coal that falls from exposed veins in the bluffs above the shoreline. Handicap-access toilets and boat launch are on-site, but no developed water source.

Be advised that especially in spring and fall extremely high tides can cover the beach. Check the local tide tables before overnighting here, particularly during those seasons. If you launch a boat into the salt water, check low-tide schedules. Boaters can encounter difficulties beaching their craft on low water. Be alert and aware concerning the weather, which can change drastically in minutes. Angling here is for Dolly Varden; steelhead trout; king, silver, red, and pink salmon. No fee; 15-day camping limit.

STARISKI CREEK STATE RECREATION SITE (Alaska State Parks)
Mile 151 Sterling Highway

A dozen or so campers can be accommodated in this sometimes crowded parking/camping area on an exceedingly high bluff. There is a fantastic view overlooking Cook Inlet to Mount Iliamna and other peaks of the Alaska Range. Well water has been developed here and there are handicap-access toilets plus picnic accommodations. You can get to the beach via 4-wheel-drive Whiskey Gulch Road. Fishing produces Dolly Varden, steelhead, and silver and pink salmon. No fee; 15-day camping limit.

ANCHOR RIVER STATE RECREATION AREA (Alaska State Parks)
Mile 157 Sterling Highway

The large parking/camping areas in this 211-acre site can accommodate 38 campers. There is no developed drinking water source but handicap-access toilets and picnic facilities are on-site.

Although beach driving sometimes looks inviting at this area, do not try it. The tide comes in swiftly here and there are sandy sink holes in the vicinity. You could get stuck and literally lose your vehicle to the incoming ocean.

Fishing here is for Dolly Varden; steelhead trout; and king, silver, and pink salmon. If you are into superlatives, drive the Anchor Point Spur Road over the bridge and down to the most westerly point in North America that can be reached by interconnected roadways! No fee; 15-day camping limit.

ANCHOR POINT STATE RECREATION SITE (Alaska State Parks)
Mile 162 Sterling Highway

This area provides a small camping area for tents only as well as another, larger area for about 9 RVs. Big rigs and trailers, however, should avoid taking the first right-hand road as you enter the site; turning around could prove difficult. Drinking water and handicap-access toilet facilities are available. Angling is for Dolly Varden; steelhead trout; and silver, pink, and king salmon. No fee; 15-day camping limit.

HOMER SPIT CAMPGROUND (private)
Located at the end of Homer Spit.

HILLSIDE PARK CAMPGROUND (city of Homer)
Mile 174 Sterling Highway
HOMER SPIT PUBLIC CAMPING AREA (city of Homer)
On Homer Spit, Mile 174 Sterling Highway.

You might want to divide your Homer visit between these spectacular city and saltwater settings. **Hillside Park Campground** is in the city proper, set on a bench knoll above much of the town. From this lofty, serene, and wooded setting, the campground offers a panoramic view of Kachemak Bay that is well worth a few hours of time and countless exposures of Kodachrome. Twenty-six campsites are established here, with toilets and 2 water sources: 1 in the campground and another at nearby ball fields.

Dump stations are available at nearby Tesoro and Union service stations. Wildlife in the area includes a delightful squirrel population and an occasional moose. There is a $4 daily fee; 14-day camping limit.

Homer Spit Public Camping Area is located on Homer Spit, an incredible, narrow gravel bar that juts nearly 5 miles into the salt waters of Kachemak Bay. The city maintains campsites in a unique 30.5-acre area of sand dunes and beach grass, with a beautiful mountain view.

Saltwater charters, restaurants, a frontier saloon, motels, seafood shops, commercial fisheries operations, and a 100-unit private camping facility are all easily accessible by a road leading down the spine of the spit.

A 5-lane boat launch on the spit guarantees no waiting. Toilets and drinking water are available. Fishing in the area is good for silver and pink salmon, Dolly Varden, bottom fish, and shellfish. Wildlife viewing includes seals, porpoises, occasional whales, eagles, and various marine birds. A daily fee of $3 is charged; camping limit is 14 days.

The Edgerton Highway and McCarthy Road (Alaska Highway 10)

This is another of Alaska's marvelous rural roads that many visitors miss, either because they are unaware of the unspoiled beauty to be found here, or they are afraid to get off the well-beaten path. (To be candid, there are some pretty steep ascents and descents along the way. Travelers pulling trailers with marginal-power vehicles may well opt to make this a day trip, leaving their rigs at some appropriate spot on the Richardson Highway.) If you make this trip, you will find precious few crowds along the likes of the Edgerton; this makes it a prime candidate for weekend or holiday travel when most Alaskans and even most visitors head for the better-known resorts.

The Edgerton is asphalt for about half of its thirty-five-mile length. Some folks prefer the gravel half to the paved surface because of frequent and substantial frost heaves. Take your time; "getting there" on this road is half the fun. The scenery is unsurpassed and ever changing. It varies from rolling hills to wide timbered valleys, grand lakes, and the imposing peaks of the Wrangell Mountains. If you are lucky you may even see buffalo herds across the Copper River. The route is downright historic: It follows roughly the path of an old gold rush pack trail between Copper Center and Chitina.

The McCarthy Road, from Chitina to McCarthy, is actually the railbed of the old (1907-38) Copper River and Northwestern Railway. This is a sixty-three-mile dirt road which, under rainy conditions, can be pretty hairy. Inquire in Chitina about the status of the road before undertaking it. We do not recommend this trip unless you are used to driving primitive roads and your vehicle will handle them. The road ends at the Copper River about one mile west of town. To get to McCarthy you have to hand-pull yourself across the river suspended on a small open tram platform. Wear gloves; you can easily injure your hands.

The Edgerton Highway has two beginning points on the Richardson Highway. The official new, paved beginning of the Edgerton commences easterly at Mile 83 on the Richardson Highway. The old Edgerton, an unpaved and still used alternative, takes off from about Mile 91 Richardson Highway. Both routes merge about twenty-five miles north of Chitina.

Following are camping opportunities along the way.

LIBERTY FALLS CAMPGROUND (Alaska State Parks)
Mile 23.5 Edgerton Highway

We believe this is just what an Alaskan campground ought to be. We overnighted with a trailer here some years back and have often relived our splendid near-isolation, our woods-enclosed campsite near a bubbling, rushing creek; and, best of all, the sight and sound of Liberty's thunderous waterfall cascading into the canyon where the campground is located.

Five camping units are located here, along with toilets and picnic facilities. Water for drinking comes from the creek, but should be boiled or treated. No fee; 7-day camping limit. Bears may be in the vicinity; be cautious if you see one.

If you are driving a really big RV, or pulling a large trailer, you may want to eyeball Liberty Falls' access road before pulling in; it is narrow in places.

Camping in Chitina is on the informal side, with RVs allowed to overnight in several areas in and around the community including Town Lake downtown. A campground is located about 2 miles west of town on McCarthy Road. Nelson's Lakeside Campground, a private facility, is operated at Sculpin Lake, Mile 12 on the McCarthy Road east of Chitina.

The Southcentral/Southwest Marine Highway

As in southeastern Alaska, there are major towns and smaller communities in southcentral and southwestern Alaska, which are served not by surface highways but by two fast, modern vessels of the Alaska state ferry system.

The larger of the two vessels is the MV *Tustumena*, a 296-foot ferry with a capacity for 220 passengers and 50 standard vehicles. Twenty-five two-berth and two four-berth cabins are available as well as reclining airline-type seating in one of the vessel's lounges, food service, a cocktail lounge, and a top-deck solarium. The *Tustumena* connects Seward, her home port, with Seldovia, Homer, Port Lions (on Kodiak Island), and Kodiak. She also sails from Seward to Valdez and Cordova on Prince William Sound. Several times each summer the vessel sails from Homer to Kodiak then to ports on the remote Alaska Peninsula and Aleutian Islands: Chignik, Sand Point, Cold Bay, and Dutch Harbor.

The MV *Bartlett* is 193 feet long with a capacity for 170 passengers and 38 vehicles. This vessel has no staterooms but does offer an observation lounge, food and cocktail service, and a top-deck solarium. The *Bartlett* sails between home-port Cordova to Valdez and Whittier in Prince William Sound, passing magnificent Columbia Glacier (and acres of icebergs disgorged from Columbia's face) in the process. Whittier is accessible by land only by a unique Alaska Railroad piggyback ride; in your vehicle secured on a railroad flatcar! Vehicles are loaded on the flatcars at Portage, which is southwest of Anchorage on the Seward Highway.

Following are communities served by the *Tustumena* and the *Bartlett*.

Seldovia

Seldovia is a quiet, secluded fishing and fish-processing community surrounded by water, woods, and gentle hills. Although it is located on the mainland just sixteen miles southwest of Homer it can be reached only by air or sea. Camping here is informal, with an undeveloped area at Outside Beach about one mile from downtown. There are picnic and toilet facilities; bring your own water.

Kodiak

Bustling Kodiak, the United State's third busiest commercial fishing center, is one of Alaska's most historic places. The Russians were here in the 1700s. It is also among the state's most beautiful regions. Huge Kodiak Island, one hundred miles long and more than thirty-six hundred square miles in area, is covered with lush forest and grasslands. It is home to the world-renowned Kodiak brown bear.

Three campgrounds, all maintained by Alaska State Parks, are located near this community. **Fort Abercrombie State Historical Park** is located at Mile 3.5 on the Mill Bay Road northeast of downtown. This area, set among abundant spruce and plant life, is a former World War II military site. Located among the fortifications and relics of that era are 14 camping units, picnic facilities, handicap-access toilets, drinking water, group shelter, trails, and access to fishing, boating, canoeing, even swimming if you are game. There are fabulous ocean views and lots of sea and shorebirds to see, but *use caution* on the sheer cliffs from which you do your sighting. A ranger station is located near the park entrance. Camping limit is 7 days.

At **Buskin River SRS**, about 2 miles southwest of downtown on the Base-Town Road, the state maintains 18 camping units along with handicap-access toilets, water, fireplaces, tables, shelter, and dump station. This site, on a lightly vegetated river outwash plain, is a good one from which to fish for salmon and Dolly Varden. Camping limit is 15 days.

Pasagshak SRS, about 45 miles from downtown on the Pasagshak Bay Road, is less developed and far more isolated. The site, surrounded on

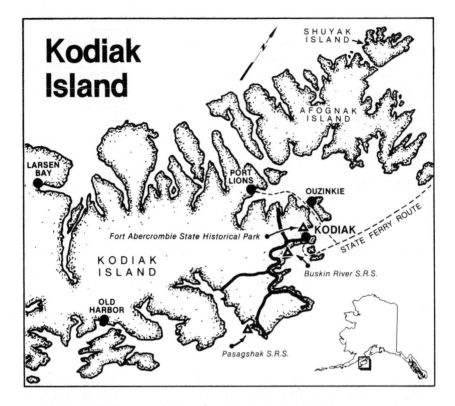

three sides by high ground, is accessed through forest land, a mountain pass, and ranch country. There are handicap-access toilets, tables, fireplaces, 7 picnic sites, and water at the area. No fee; 15-day camping limit.

The newly created **Shuyak Island State Park**, accessible by air (about a 30-minute flight from Kodiak) has 4 public-use cabins that can be rented for $15 per person per night. For information, call (907) 486-6339 or write to Alaska State Parks, Area Superintendent, SR Box 3800, Kodiak, Alaska 99615.

Here is another fly-in opportunity. There are no roads within the 1,865,000-acre **Kodiak National Wildlife Refuge** on Kodiak Island and nearby Afognak Island, therefore travel is limited to easily chartered floatplanes. Public-use recreation cabins are available in the refuge. For details and reservation information contact the Kodiak National Wildlife Refuge Manager, Box 825, Kodiak, Alaska 99615.

Whittier

The little community of Whittier lies at the base of massive, snow- and glacier-capped mountains. The city is accessible only by air, rail, and by Alaska state ferry. There are no developed campgrounds in the community, however self-contained RVs can park in the surrounding area. Most of Whittier's 260-odd residents live in the tall, imposing, seemingly incongruous Begich Towers, which were United States military structures during World War II. Now they are condos. Fishing and sightseeing charter boats are available in the community, as are restaurants and inns.

Cordova

Scenically situated on the shores of Orca Inlet in island-studded Prince William Sound and surrounded by mountains and forests, the city of Cordova is today one of southcentral Alaska's principal fishing and fish-processing centers. Half a century ago is was the saltwater terminus of the now-defunct Copper River and Northwestern Railway from the Kennecott copper mines at McCarthy and Kennicott. Four roadside camping areas are available in the area.

Odiak Campground (city of Cordova) is within .5 mile of downtown, located next to the community's former garbage dump (now mercifully closed). Showers, water, and toilets are on-site. There is a nominal fee.

Hartney Bay Recreation Area (private) is located about 7 miles southwest of downtown Cordova on the Whitshed Road. Owner-operator of the campground is Eyak Corporation, one of the Alaska Native corporations established by the United States congressional Alaska Native Claims Settlement Act. For a permit to camp here, contact Eyak Corporation at 424-7161.

At Mile 12 on the Copper River Highway leading east of town, a 3-mile access road leads to **Cabin Lake Recreation Area,** another private facility under the jurisdiction of the Eyak Corporation.

At Mile 17 Copper River Highway, a 3-mile road leads to **Alaganik Slough Campground (USFS).** Facilities include a parking/camping area for RVs and tents, toilets, picnic facilities, and a boat launch. Here, and along the Copper River delta to the east and north, are found the greatest concentrations anywhere of formerly endangered trumpeter swans. These incredibly beautiful creatures have a wingspan of six to eight feet. Caution: This area contains a heavy bear population; if you see one, keep your distance.

In addition to roadside camping and picnic facilities, the USFS maintains a number of public-use fly-in cabins on nearby lakes and beaches. Rental fee is $15 per night per cabin. For maps, details, or reservations see the USDA Forest Service, Cordova Ranger District, 334 Fourth Avenue, Cordova, Alaska 99574 or call (907) 271-2599. For information by mail write to United States Forest Service, Chugach National Forest, 201 East Ninth Avenue, Suite 206, Anchorage, Alaska 99501.

Visitor campgrounds, as such, do not exist at the other communities served by the Southwest ferry segment: Port Lions, Chignik, Sand Point, King Cove, Cold Bay, and Dutch Harbor. That is not to say that truly adventurous RVers could not visit and enjoy these locations, but they would be strictly on their own and would have to inquire at each location as to the best location for parking and overnighting.

For a listing of campgrounds in and around the ferry ports of Seward and Valdez, see pages 147–148 and 120 respectively.

7

Loose Ends

In this final chapter we will tie up any loose ends by providing you with additional sources of Alaska and Yukon travel information; suggest some additional books about the North Country; and, very important if the need arises, we list telephone numbers to call in case of emergency.

Additional Travel Information

Following are government and private agencies that will send you additional information about travel to and through the North Country.

Alaska Division of Tourism, Box E, Juneau, Alaska 99811

Alaska Department of Fish and Game, Box 3-2000, Juneau, Alaska 99802-2000

Alaska Marine Highway System, Box R, Juneau, Alaska 99811

Alaska Wilderness Guides Association, Box 89061, Anchorage, Alaska 99508

British Columbia Ferries, 818 Broughton Street, Victoria, British Columbia, Canada V8W 1E4

North by Northwest Tourism Association of British Columbia, Box 1030, Smithers, British Columbia, Canada V0J 2NO

Northwest Territories Department of Economic Development and Tourism, Government of Northwest Territories, Inuvik, Northwest Territories, Canada X0E 0T0

Southeast Alaska Tourism Council, Box 385, Juneau, Alaska 99802

Tourism British Columbia, Box C-34971, Seattle, Washington 98124-1971

Tourism Yukon, Box 2703, Whitehorse, Yukon Territory, Canada Y1A 2C6

TravelArctic, Yellowknife, Northwest Territories, Canada X1A 2L9

Yukon Association of Wilderness Guides, Box 4768, Whitehorse, Yukon Territory, Canada Y1A 4Z2

Western Arctic Visitors Association, Box 1525, Inuvik, Northwest Territories, Canada X0E 0T0

Books About Alaska and the Yukon Territory

Obviously, the more you know about this splendid land in advance of your journey, the more you will appreciate and enjoy it once you get here. We recommend the following books.

Alaska's Southeast by Sarah Eppenbach, Pacific Search Press, 222 Dexter Avenue North, Seattle, Washington 98109 ($11.95 plus $1.00 postage). This is, in our opinion, the best, most interestingly written guide to southeastern Alaska you can buy. History, Native cultures, and wildlife as well as sites, cities, towns, and tiny villages all come dramatically alive in this nearly 300-page book.

The MILEPOST®, Alaska Northwest Publishing Company, 130 Second Avenue South, Edmonds, Washington 98020 ($14.95 plus $1.00 postage). Mile by mile through British Columbia, Yukon Territory, and Alaska, plus Alberta and the Northwest Territories, *The MILEPOST®* lists virtually every town, settlement, geologic feature, and travel accommodation along the highways, flyways, and ferry routes of the North Country in its 500-plus pages. An excellent reference, along with this book, to take with you on your journey.

Alaska's Parklands, The Complete Guide by Nancy Lange Simmerman, The Mountaineers-Books, 715 Pike Street, Seattle, Washington 98101 ($13.95). With the passage of the 1980 Alaska National Interest Lands Conservation Act, the United States Congress set aside more than 104 million acres of federal parks, preserves, national monuments, and wild and scenic rivers for protection and preservation in Alaska. These parks are in addition to the not-inconsequential hundreds of thousands of acres of lands already in state parks status. In this 336-page book, Nancy Simmerman describes each of Alaska's parklands: state and federal lands, remote seldom-visited sites, as well as the popular crowd-pleasers along the highways. She tells about terrain, wildlife, scientific value, and trails within each park. If you are especially interested in the rugged, remote campsites, this is the book you need.

In addition to the books listed above, the following publications also will provide valuable information to enhance your northern vacation.

Adventuring in Alaska by Peggy Wayburn, Sierra Club Books, 530 Bush Street, San Francisco, California 94108 ($10.95 plus $2.50 postage).

Remote lodges, camping places, and wilderness expeditions.

Alaska's Backcountry Hideaways—Southcentral by Roberta L. Graham, Pacific Search Press, 222 Dexter Avenue North, Seattle, Washington 98109 ($10.95 plus $1.00 postage). This 144-page book is a traveler's guide to more than fifty great hideaway retreats, road lodges, and remote public-use cabins, from the Kenai Peninsula to the Arctic Circle.

Alaska. Subscription office: *Alaska* Magazine, Depot Square, Peterborough, New Hampshire 03458-9950 ($21.00 for one year, 12 issues). For more than fifty years this has been Alaska's principal magazine of Life on the Last Frontier.

Alaska Travel Guide, Box 15889, Salt Lake City, Utah 84115 ($9.95 plus $2.00 postage). An excellent 500-page mile-by-mile guide to highway attractions and accommodations.

Facts About Alaska, the Alaska Almanac, Alaska Northwest Publishing Company, 130 Second Avenue South, Edmonds, Washington 98020 ($5.95 plus $1.00 postage). Facts, figures, historical notes, and statistics about the forty-ninth state.

Fifty-five Ways to the Wilderness in Southcentral Alaska by Helen Nienhueser and Nancy Simmerman, The Mountaineers, 300 3rd West, Seattle, Washington 98101 ($9.95). Trails, routes, and remote sites you can hike in Alaska's southcentral region.

Fodor's Alaska by Norma Spring, Fodor's Travel Guides, New York, New York ($8.95). Small enough to fit in glove compartment or purse, yet it covers travel and attractions in every region of the state. For decades, Norma Spring has been covering Alaska interestingly, accurately, and with great enthusiasm.

Inside Passage Traveler by Ellen Searby, Windham Bay Press, Box 021332, Juneau, Alaska 99802 ($7.95 postpaid or add $1.50 for airmail). This book is full of practical where-to, how-to, how-much information for ferry travelers from Seattle to the top of the southeastern Alaska panhandle.

Emergency Medical Services

The office of Emergency Medical Services of the Division of Public Health, Alaska Department of Health and Social Services, has compiled the following list of telephone numbers to call in case of a medical emergency. The list covers all the highways of the state of Alaska, the Alaska Marine Highway system, and the principal highways of the Yukon Territory. Be aware that every vessel of the Alaska Marine Highway system has an Emergency Trauma Technician on staff. If you become sick or injured while traveling aboard a state ferry, contact the ship's purser and he will arrange for treatment.

ALASKA MARINE HIGHWAY
Southeast

Angoon: Emergency 788-3631 (public safety); Angoon Health Center 788-3524.
Haines: Emergency 911; Haines Health Center 766-2125.
Hollis: Emergency 862-3330 (Craig police); Hollis Health Center (no phone).
Hoonah: Emergency 945-3655 (police); Hoonah Health Center 945-3235.
Juneau: Emergency 911; Bartlett Memorial Hospital 586-8427.
Kake: Emergency 785-3393 (police); Kake Health Center 785-3333.
Ketchikan: Emergency 911; Ketchikan General Hospital 225-5171.
Metlakatla: Emergency 911; Alaska Native Health Clinic 866-4741.
Pelican: Emergency 735-2207 (public safety); Pelican Health Center 735-2250.
Petersburg: Emergency 911; Petersburg General Hospital 772-4291.
Sitka: Emergency 911; Sitka Community Hospital 747-3241.
Skagway: Emergency 983-2300 (fire department); Skagway Health Center 983-2255.
Wrangell: Emergency 2000; Wrangell General Hospital 874-3356.

ALASKA MARINE HIGHWAY
Southcentral

Cordova: Emergency 911; Cordova Community Hospital 424-7551.
Homer: Emergency 911; South Peninsula Hospital 235-8101.
Seldovia: Emergency 234-7800; Seldovia Medical Clinic 234-7825.
Seward: Emergency 911; Seward General Hospital 224-5205.
Valdez: Emergency 911; Valdez Community Hospital 835-2249.
Whittier: Emergency 911; Whittier Clinic 472-2303.

ALASKA MARINE HIGHWAY
Kodiak Island

Kodiak: Emergency 911; Kodiak Island Hospital 486-3281.
Port Lions: Emergency 454-2909 (public safety); clinic 454-2101.

ALASKA MARINE HIGHWAY
Aleutian Islands

Chignik: Emergency 749-2233 (clinic); city 749-2273.
Cold Bay: Emergency 532-2453 (flight service); health center 532-2413.

Dutch

Harbor: Emergency 911; Illiuliuk Clinic 581-1202 or 581-1203.

King Cove: Emergency 211 (police); King Cove Medical Clinic
           497-2311.

Sand Point: Emergency 911; Sand Point Medical Clinic 383-3151.

ALASKA HIGHWAY
Dawson Creek, British Columbia, to Delta Junction, Alaska

KM 0 (Dawson Creek) to
KM 38 (Kiskatinaw Park)
Provincial Ambulance Service at KM 0
Phone 782-2211

KM 38 (past Kiskatinaw Park) to
KM 162 (Wonowon)
Provincial Ambulance Service
(Fort Saint John) at KM 75
Phone 785-2079

KM 162 (Wonowon) to
KM 363 (Bougie Creek Bridge)
Provincial Ambulance Service
(Pink Mountain) at KM 228
Phone 772-3234 *or* JJ36397 radiophone

KM 363 (Bougie Creek Bridge) to
KM 631 (Summit Lake)
Provincial Ambulance Service
(Fort Nelson) at KM 460
Phone 774-6919

KM 622 (Summit Lake) to
KM 800 (Liard River)
Provincial Ambulance Service
(Toad River) at KM 674
Phone 232-5351

KM 800 (Liard River) to
KM 946 (British Columbia-Yukon Territory border)
Provincial Ambulance Service
(Coal River) at KM 859
Phone 776-3306

KM 946 (British Columbia-Yukon Territory border) to
KM 1180 (Swift River)
Watson Lake Ambulance at KM 1017
Phone 536-7355 *or* 536-7443 (Royal Canadian Mounted Police)

KM 1180 (Swift River) to
KM 1366 (Squanga Lake)
Teslin Ambulance at KM 1293
Phone 390-2510 *or* 390-2500 (RCMP)

KM 1366 (Squanga Lake) to
KM 1558 (Mendenhall)
Whitehorse Ambulance at KM 1474
Phone 668-9333

KM 1558 (Mendenhall) to
KM 1700 (near Kluane Lake Lodge)
Haines Junction at KM 1635
Phone 634-2213 *or* 634-2221 (RCMP)

KM 1700 (near Kluane Lake Lodge) to
KM 1860 (Longs Creek)
Destruction Bay at KM 1742
Phone 841-4151 *or* 841-4161 (RCMP)

KM 1860 (Longs Creek) to
KM 1968 (Yukon Territory-Alaska border)
Beaver Creek at KM 1934
Phone 862-7300 (RCMP) *or* 862-7230 (Canada customs)

MP 1221 (Alaska-Yukon Territory border) to
MP 1314 (Tok)
Northway Emergency Services 7 miles south of MP 1264
Phone 778-2211

MP 1221 (Alaska-Yukon Territory border) to
MP 1314 (Tok)
Port Alcan Rescue Team
Phone 778-6842 *or* 778-6252 (Alaska customs)

MP 1221 (Alaska-Yukon Territory border) to
MP 1361 (Dot Lake)
Tok Ambulance at MP 1314
Phone 883-5111 (state troopers) *or* 778-6252 (Alaska customs)

MP 1361 (Dot Lake) to
MP 1422 (end of Alaska Highway)
Delta Rescue at MP 265.5 Richardson Highway
Phone 895-4600 (24-hour dispatch) *or* 895-4800 (state troopers)

CHENA HOT SPRINGS ROAD
MP 5 Steese Highway to Chena Hot Springs

MP 0 (Steese Highway junction) to
MP 52 (Chena Hot Springs)
Interior Ambulance Rescue Squad
Phone 911 *or* 452-1313 (state troopers)

DALTON HIGHWAY
North Slope Haul Road

MP 0 (junction with Elliott Highway) to
MP 30
Livengood Emergency Medical Squad
CB channels 9, 14, 19; ask for relay to state troopers

MP 30 to
MP 210.8 (Disaster Creek)
Alaska State Troopers
CB channel 19; ask for relay to state troopers *or* ask for a message to be
    relayed to the guard at any Alyeska facility or to any state department
    of transportation facility. They can contact state troopers.

DENALI HIGHWAY
Paxson to Cantwell

MP 0 (Paxson) to
MP 78 (Susitna River)
Copper River Emergency Medical Squad
Phone 822-3203 *or* 768-2202 (state troopers)

MP 78 (Susitna River) to
MP 135 (Cantwell)
Cantwell Ambulance at MP 132.5
Phone 768-2982 *or* 768-2240 (fire department) *or* 768-2202 (state troopers)

EDGERTON HIGHWAY/McCARTHY ROAD
MP 83 Richardson Highway to McCarthy

MP 0 (Richardson Highway junction) to
MP 63 McCarthy Road (McCarthy)
Copper River Emergency Medical Services (Glennallen)
Phone 822-3203 *or* 911

ELLIOTT HIGHWAY
Fox to Manley Hot Springs

MP 0 (Fox) to
MP 32 (borough boundary)
Interior Ambulance Rescue Squad
Phone 911 *or* 452-1313 (state troopers)

MP 32 (borough boundary) to
MP 152 (Manley Hot Springs)
Phone 911 *or* 452-1313 (state troopers)

MP 44 (Tatalina River) to
MP 94 (Ptarmigan Hill)
Livengood Emergency Medical Squad at MP 77
Phone 911 *or* 452-1313 (state troopers) *or* CB channels 9, 14, 19; ask for
    relay to troopers.

GEORGE PARKS HIGHWAY
Glenn Highway junction to Fairbanks

MP 35.3 (Glenn Highway junction) to
MP 52.3 (Big Lake Road junction)
Wasilla Ambulance at MP 42.3
Phone 911

MP 52.3 (Big Lake Road junction) to
MP 64.5 (Nancy Lake Marina)
Houston Ambulance at MP 57.4
Phone 911

MP 64.5 (Nancy Lake Marina) to
MP 91
Willow Volunteer Ambulance at MP 71
Phone 911

MP 91 to
MP 104.3 (Big Susitna River)
Susitna Ambulance at MP 14.5 Talkeetna Spur Road
Phone 911 *or* 733-2256

MP 104.3 (Big Susitna River) to
MP 200 (Mat-Su borough boundary at Summit)
Trapper Creek Ambulance at MP 114.5
Phone 911 *or* 733-2256 (state troopers)

MP 174 (Hurricane Gulch) to
MP 224 (Carlo Creek)
Cantwell Ambulance at MP 210
Phone 768-2982 *or* 768-2240 (fire department) *or* 768-2202 (state
    troopers)

MP 224 (Carlo Creek) to
MP 276 (Rex Bridge)
Tri-Valley Fire Department at MP 248.9
Phone 911 *or* 683-2232 (state troopers)

MP 250 (Dry Creek Bridge) to
MP 330 (Swede's Place)
Nenana Fire Department at MP 304
Phone 911

MP 330 (Swede's Place) to
MP 356 (Sheep Creek Road)
Chena/Goldstream Volunteer Fire Department
Phone 911

MP 356 (Sheep Creek Road) to
MP 358 (city of Fairbanks)
University of Alaska Fire Department
Phone 911

GLENN HIGHWAY
Anchorage to Glennallen

MP 0 (city of Anchorage) to
MP 13.6 (Eagle River)
Anchorage Fire Department at MP 13.6
Phone 911; CB channel 9, REACT

MP 13.6 (Eagle River) to
MP 30.8 (Knik River Bridge) (old and new Glenn Highways)
Chugiak Volunteer Fire and Rescue
Phone 911 *or* 688-2555; CB channel 18

MP 30.8 (Knik River Bridge) to
MP 54.5 (Moose Creek)
Palmer Ambulance Service at MP 41.5
Phone 911

MP 52 (Moose Creek) to
MP 120 (Eureka)
Sutton Ambulance Service at MP 61
Phone 911

MP 128 (Eureka Lodge) to
MP 189 (Richardson Highway junction)
Copper River Emergency Medical Services at MP 187
Phone 911 *or* 822-3203

Note: The Glenn Highway continues to Tok, with a 14-mile link via the
Richardson Highway plus the 125-mile Tok Cutoff.

HAINES HIGHWAY
Haines, Alaska, to Haines Junction, Yukon Territory

MP 0 (Haines) to
MP 40/KM 72 (Alaska-Canada border)
Phone 911

KM 72/MP 40 (Alaska-Canada border) to
KM 256 (Haines Junction)
Haines Junction Ambulance at KM 256
Phone 634-2213 *or* 634-2221 (RCMP)

KENAI SPUR ROAD
Sterling Highway junction/Soldotna Y to end of road

MP 0 (outside Kenai) to
MP 4 (Kenai city limits)
Central Peninsula Emergency Medical Services
Phone 911

MP 4 (Kenai city limits) to
MP 15 (Kenai city limits)
Kenai Fire Department at MP 11
Phone 911

MP 15 (Kenai city limits) to
MP 41 (end of road, plus all side roads and platforms in the upper inlet)
Nikiski Fire Department at MP 17.9 and MP 26.8
Phone 911

KLONDIKE HIGHWAY
Skagway to Dawson City and
TOP OF THE WORLD HIGHWAY
Dawson City to Alaska border

MP 0 (Skagway) to
MP 27/KM 44 (railroad crossing)
Skagway Fire Department at MP 0
Phone (907) 983-2300

KM 44 (railroad crossing) to
KM 141 (Annie Lake Road)
Carcross Ambulance at KM 105
Phone (403) 821-3341 *or* 821-3141

KM 141 (Annie Lake Road) to
KM 281 (Braeburn Lodge)
Whitehorse Ambulance at KM 178
Phone (403) 668-9333

KM 281 (Braeburn Lodge) to
KM 465 (Pelly Crossing)
Carmacks Ambulance at KM 357
Phone 863-5501 *or* 863-5251 (RCMP)

KM 465 (Pelly Crossing) to
KM 590 (McQuesten River Lodge)
Mayo Ambulance
Phone 996-2345 *or* 996-2322 (RCMP)

KM 590 (McQuesten River Lodge) to
Alaska border (67 miles past Dawson City)
Dawson City Ambulance at KM 718
Phone 993-5333 *or* 993-5444 (RCMP)

NABESNA ROAD
MP 59.6 Tok Cutoff to Nabesna

MP 0 (Tok Cutoff junction) to
MP 45 (Nabesna)
Copper River Emergency Medical Services (Glennallen)
Phone 911 *or* 822-3203

OLD GLENN HIGHWAY
MP 29.6 junction Glenn Highway to Palmer

MP 0 (junction Glenn Highway) to
MP 11
Butte Ambulance Service at MP 6
Phone 911

MP 11 to
MP 18.6 (Arctic Avenue junction in Palmer)
Phone 911

RICHARDSON HIGHWAY
Valdez to Fairbanks

MP 0 (Valdez) to
MP 60 (large turnout)
Valdez Volunteer Fire Department at MP 0
Phone 911

MP 60 (large turnout) to
MP 185 (Denali Highway junction)
Copper River Emergency Medical Services (Glennallen)
Phone 822-3203 *or* 911

MP 185 (Denali Highway junction) to
MP 310 (Birch Lake)
Delta Rescue Squad at MP 265.5
Phone 895-4600 (24-hour dispatch) *or* 895-4800 (state troopers)

MP 310 (Birch Lake) to
MP 341 (Eielson Air Force Base main gate)
Salcha Rescue
Phone 911

MP 341 (Eielson Air Force Base main gate) to
MP 359 (Badger Road-Fairbanks city limits)
North Pole Fire Department
Phone 911

SEWARD HIGHWAY
Anchorage to Seward

MP 127 (downtown Anchorage) to
MP 75.2 (municipality of Anchorage boundary)
Anchorage Fire Department
Phone 911

MP 110 (Beluga Point) to
MP 75.2 (municipality of Anchorage boundary)
Anchorage Fire Department at MP 90 (Girdwood)
Phone 911 *or* 783-2911

MP 75.2 to
MP 52 (near Hope Road junction)
Hope/Sunrise Emergency Medical Services
Phone 786-3601; CB channel 9

MP 55 (including Hope Road) to
MP 30 (Moose Pass)
Cooper Landing Volunteer Ambulance
Phone 911 *or* 595-1255 *or* Summit Lake Lodge (MP 46) can relay
    emergency messages 24 hours a day via radio to Cooper Landing
    Volunteer Ambulance.

MP 30 (Moose Pass) to
MP 0 (downtown Seward)
Bear Creek Rescue at MP 6
Phone 911 *or* 224-3344

MP 30 (Moose Pass) to
MP 0 (downtown Seward)
Seward Volunteer Ambulance at MP 0
Phone 911 *or* 224-3338

STEESE HIGHWAY
Fairbanks to Circle

MP 2 (old Steese Highway) to
MP 86 (borough boundary/12 Mile Summit)
Interior Ambulance Rescue Squad
Phone 911 *or* 452-1313 (state troopers)

MP 22 to
MP 45
Chatanika Emergency Response Team
Phone 911 *or* 452-1313 (state troopers) *or* Old F. E. Company Camp
(MP 27) can relay emergency messages via radio.

MP 86 (borough boundary/12 Mile Summit) to
MP 110
Phone 911 *or* 452-1313 (state troopers)

MP 110 to
MP 162 (Circle)
Central Emergency Team
Phone 911 *or* 452-1313 (state troopers) *or* CB channels 2, 19, 22 and ask for
relay to troopers.

STERLING HIGHWAY
Seward Highway junction to Homer

MP 38 (Seward Highway junction) to
MP 59 (Skilak Lake Loop Road junction)
Cooper Landing Volunteer Ambulance
Phone 911 *or* 595-1257

MP 59 (Skilak Lake Loop Road junction) to
MP 121 (White Alice Tower plus all roads within that area)
Central Peninsula Emergency Medical Services at MP 94
Phone 911

MP 121 (White Alice Tower) to
MP 145 (Happy Valley)
Ninilchik Volunteer Ambulance at MP 136
Phone 911

MP 145 (Happy Valley) to
MP 170 (near historic view of Kachemak Bay)
Anchor Point Volunteer Fire Department at MP 156.5
Phone 911

MP 145 (Happy Valley) to
MP 179 (end of Homer Spit plus East End Road to 20 Mile and all
    accessible back roads)
Homer Volunteer Fire Department at MP 174
Phone 911

TAYLOR HIGHWAY
Tetlin Junction to Eagle

MP 0 (Tetlin Junction) to
MP 113 (O'Brien Creek Bridge)
Tok Ambulance at MP 1314 Alaska Highway
Phone 883-5111 (state troopers)

MP 113 (O'Brien Creek Bridge) to
MP 161 (Eagle)
Phone 452-1313 *or* 452-2114 (state troopers)

TOK CUTOFF
Richardson Highway junction to Tok

MP 0 (Richardson Highway Junction) to
MP 63 (Duffy's)
Copper River Emergency Medical Services (Glennallen)
Phone 911 *or* 822-3203

MP 63 (Duffy's) to
MP 125 (Tok)
Tok Ambulance Service at MP 125
Phone 883-5111 (state troopers)

Note: CB channels 9 and 11 are monitored for emergencies in most areas on the highways in Alaska. In some areas CB channels 14 and 19 are monitored. Most truckers monitor channel 19. All emergency access numbers listed here are available twenty-four hours a day, unless otherwise noted. In Canada, if you do not get a response when calling an RCMP number, dial 0 and ask the operator for Zenith 5000.

Index

SELECTED BOOKS FROM PACIFIC SEARCH PRESS

Cooking

American Wood Heat Cookery (2d Ed. Revised & Enlarged) by
Margaret Byrd Adams
The Apple Cookbook by Kyle D. Fulwiler
The Bean Cookbook: Dry Legume Cookery by Norma S. Upson
The Berry Cookbook (2d Ed. Revised & Enlarged) by Kyle D. Fulwiler
Canning and Preserving without Sugar (Updated) by Norma M.
MacRae, R.D.
The Eating Well Cookbook by John Doerper
Eating Well: A Guide to Foods of the Pacific Northwest by John Doerper
The Eggplant Cookbook by Norma S. Upson
A Fish Feast by Charlotte Wright
Food 101: A Student Guide to Quick and Easy Cooking by Cathy Smith
Kayak Cookery: A Handbook of Provisions and Recipes by Linda Daniel
One Potato, Two Potato: A Cookbook by Constance Bollen and Marlene
Blessing
River Runners' Recipes by Patricia Chambers
The Salmon Cookbook by Jerry Dennon
Shellfish Cookery: Absolutely Delicious Recipes from the West Coast by
John Doerper
Starchild & Holahan's Seafood Cookbook by Adam Starchild and James
Holahan
Wild Mushroom Recipes by Puget Sound Mycological Society
The Zucchini Cookbook (3rd Ed. Revised & Enlarged) by Paula
Simmons

Crafts

The Chilkat Dancing Blanket by Cheryl Samuel
The Guide to Successful Tapestry Weaving by Nancy Harvey
An Illustrated Guide to Making Oriental Rugs by Gordon W. Scott
Patterns for Tapestry Weaving: Projects and Techniques by Nancy
Harvey
Spinning and Weaving with Wool (Updated) by Paula Simmons

Health

A Practical Guide to Independent Living for Older People by Alice H.
Phillips and Caryl K. Roman

Nature

The Birdhouse Book: Building Houses, Feeders, and Baths by Don McNeil
Growing Organic Vegetables West of the Cascades by Steve Solomon
Marine Mammals of Eastern North Pacific and Arctic Waters (2d Ed. Revised) edited by Delphine Haley
Seabirds of Eastern North Pacific and Arctic Waters edited by Delphine Haley

Northwest Scene

At the Forest's Edge: Memoir of a Physician-Naturalist by David Tirrell Hellyer
The Pike Place Market: People, Politics, and Produce by Alice Shorett and Murray Morgan
Seattle Photography by David Barnes
The Seattle GuideBook (6th Ed. Revised & Enlarged) by Archie Satterfield
They Tried to Cut It All by Edwin Van Syckle

Outdoor Recreation

Cross-Country Downhill and Other Nordic Mountain Skiing Techniques (3d Ed. Revised & Enlarged) by Steve Barnett
The Coastal Kayaker: Kayak Camping on the Alaska and B.C. Coast by Randel Washburne
Derek C. Hutchinson's Guide to Sea Kayaking by Derek C. Hutchinson
Fundamentals of Kayak Navigation by David Burch
Kayak Trips in Puget Sound and the San Juan Islands by Randel Washburne
River Runners' Recipes by Patricia Chambers
The White-Water River Book: A Guide to Techniques, Equipment, Camping, and Safety by Ron Watters/Robert Winslow, photography
Whitewater Trips for Kayakers, Canoeists, and Rafters in British Columbia, Greater Vancouver through Whistler and Thompson River Regions by Betty Pratt-Johnson
Whitewater Trips for Kayakers, Canoeists, and Rafters on Vancouver Island by Betty Pratt-Johnson

Travel

Alaska's Backcountry Hideaways: Southcentral by Roberta L. Graham

Alaska's Southeast: Touring the Inside Passage (2d Ed. Revised & Enlarged) by Sarah Eppenbach

The Bed and Breakfast Traveler: Touring the West Coast by Lewis Green

Cruising the Columbia and Snake Rivers (2d Ed. Revised & Enlarged) by Sharlene P. and Ted W. Nelson and Joan LeMieux

Cruising the Pacific Coast, Acapulco to Skagway (4th Ed. Revised) by Carolyn and Jack West

The Getaway Guide I: Short Vacations in the Pacific Northwest (2d Ed. Revised & Enlarged) by Marni and Jake Rankin

The Getaway Guide II: More Short Vacations in the Pacific Northwest (2d Ed. Revised & Enlarged) by Marni and Jake Rankin

The Getaway Guide III: Short Vacations in Northern California by Marni and Jake Rankin

The Getaway Guide IV: Short Vacations in Southern California by Marni and Jake Rankin

Journey to the High Southwest: A Traveler's Guide (2d Ed. Revised) by Robert Casey